THE GAME MATTERS

Jasmine,
Thank you for your
kind hospitality!
All my Best,

INSIGHT PUBLISHING
SEVIERVILLE, TENNESSEE

© 2005 by Insight Publishing Company.

All rights reserved. No part of this book may be reproduced in any form or by any means without prior written permission from the publisher except for brief quotations embodied in critical essay, article, or review. These articles and/or reviews must state the correct title and contributing author of this book by name.

Published by Insight Publishing Company
P.O. Box 4189
Sevierville, Tennessee 37864

10 9 8 7 6 5 4 3 2

Printed in The United States

ISBN: 1-932863-62-1

Table Of Contents

A Message From The Publisher

Some say that sport is a microcosm of life in general—people working as individuals or teams competing for rewards or self-satisfaction. Men and women who have competed in a sport learn valuable lessons that impact their success in business. They learn goal setting, discipline, sacrifice, and teamwork. They learn to put winning and losing in perspective and how to bounce back from defeat. They are forced to co-exist and even thrive alongside people they didn't necessarily choose to be their teammate. And they learn the sweet taste of victory, knowing that all their hard work has a significant reward.

The men and women featured in this edition of, *The Game Matters*, offer a wellspring of advice based on their experience in the world of sports. Every person who reads this book will take away valuable insights that, when applied, will make a genuine difference in their lives!

Interviews conducted by:

David E. Wright
President, International Speakers Network

Chapter One

Steve Garvey

THE INTERVIEW

David E. Wright (Wright)

It's my pleasure today to visit with Mr. Steve Garvey. As one of the most successful major league baseball players of all time, Steve is the reigning national league "Iron Man" fifteen years following his retirement from baseball. The man who once played in 1,207 consecutive baseball games has utilized that same drive and leadership to motivate audiences around the world to become the best and the most successful people or corporations they can become.

Steve Garvey's playing field has changed from the baseball diamond to corporate boardrooms and lecture halls, but the integrity, the intensity, and the devotion for which this future Hall of Famer is famous for is the same.

Steve, welcome to our program, *The Game Matters*!

Steve Garvey (Garvey)

It's my pleasure. It's nice to be with you.

Wright

As an athlete you've achieved success at the highest level—the Major Leagues. You won a World Series Title with the Los Angeles

Dodgers, you were named the Most Valuable Player of the National League and you were on the All Star Team on ten different occasions. You were named MVP in two All Star games and playoff MPV three times. Thinking back to your days in college at Michigan State, did you dream about this kind of success or did you have some kind of plan to achieve it?

Garvey

Well, that's a very good question because once you get to college and you're having a certain amount of success there, Major League professional regional scouts are scouting you. You know that you're in the radarscope, so to speak; but I think in college, you're just trying to do your best, the very best you can. You're also trying to do help your team be successful—possibly go to the Regionals and the College World Series (although we unfortunately just missed that at Michigan State).

During my sophomore year we had seen numerous scouts in the stands at Iowa, Minnesota, and Michigan. I had been told that I was probably going to go in the first two rounds.

I started to think about being a professional baseball player—I had dreamed of it, somewhat but not a lot. I always thought I needed to really concentrate and work hard to develop my skills if I thought I'd have a chance at becoming a professional.

After my sophomore year at Michigan State—I had been All American third baseman—I went home either June first or second. The next morning the *Tampa Tribune* had my picture on the front page with the headline, "Garvey drafted by the Dodgers." That was really a dream come true. I had been a batboy for the Dodgers in spring training beginning when I was about seven through age twelve. (At that time my dad drove the bus for Greyhound.) Being drafted by the Dodgers was the first stage of my dream coming true. Little do they know *I* would have paid *them* to sign, but—.

Wright

I won't tell them if you won't!

Garvey

With the few extra dollars and a new car and the rest of my education, we really made out, so that worked well.

Wright

In our book, *The Game Matters,* we're hoping to inspire people from all walks of life to reach for big dreams and achieve them by understanding and applying proven success principles from the world of sports. In your case, I'd like to start at the very beginning. What was life like for you growing up—what did you learn as a young person about success that helped you in the Major Leagues?

Garvey

I was an only child with two hard-working parents. I grew up in Tampa, Florida. My mom and dad were originally from Long Island, New York, and moved to Tampa when my grandfather on my mother's side had swapped a gas station for a motel. He said, "Let's go to Florida. Let's get out of the cold New York weather."

The motel business lasted about a year and a half. I was born during that time and both of my grandparents and my parents decided to remain in Tampa. I was the type of kid who just loved sports. At that time sports was a seasonal activity—you went from football in the fall to basketball in the winter to baseball in the spring—the the various kinds of sports didn't overlap then as much as they do now. Around that time—in the mid '50s—Little League came on the scene.

My dad and about three other gentlemen started the second Little League team in Tampa, Florida, and I may have started a year sooner than was usually allowed. They needed some players, so I ended up in right field standing in the puddles, stopping the ball with my foot or throwing my glove at it, then tossing it back in.

By the time I was nine or ten, I think the game took over somehow and with my God-given talent I started to become successful in Little League. By the time I was twelve I had hit twenty homeruns in eighteen games, I had thrown three no-hitters in a row, and I was really dominating my League at that time for a boy my age.

As I look back, probably the foundation of my success is the caring, the sharing, the discipline, the laws and the many things my parents taught me—the good sound principles of being a responsible individual. This included showing up for every practice. I was a good teammate, doing everything I could to help my teammates be better, and fulfilling the role I was given—either pitching or shortstop, and batting. I think most of the ideas and principles we take with us into adulthood are formulated when we were kids from probably seven through fifteen or sixteen. I believe our work ethics are very, very important. Work ethics weren't taught to me as much verbally as by example by my parents. Both parents worked extremely hard. My mother was a secretary for an insurance company and my dad, as I mentioned before, drove a bus for Greyhound. They worked very, very hard. Just their example made me want to go to school every day and do the best I could and then on the playing fields do the best I could do.

Wright

Were you influenced in any other significant ways as a child?

Garvey

When I was nine my grandfather passed away (he was the one who had traded the gas station for the motel) and my grandmother was a semi-invalid. She had a rare neurological disease that allowed her to walk, but she couldn't use her arms or hands--they were very stiff. She moved in with us and I was responsible for helping her in various ways. When school was over, I would come home and help start dinner. Mom and Dad would usually come home about 5:00 p.m., and Grandmother then let me run and play. When she turned the porch light on I knew that was my signal to come on in—she needed me.

I would have to do a lot of things for her, but she was such an inspiration to me. Even with her inability to use her arms and hands, she would still vacuum—she would put the little vacuum pole between her arms and push it around. She had a way of ironing where she'd get the ironing board and set it up. She then would take a shirt and put it on the top of the ironing board and move the shirt with her teeth as she pushed the iron around. She'd then push the iron onto a pan and use her teeth to move the shirt again. As a young man this made an impact on me. Responsibility for my grandmother was not just an added responsibility that I really cared about and that I wanted to do. Having a close relative like her who was disabled but who would do what she could because she wanted to make her contribution to the family was a positive influence on me. I think she had a tremendous influence on me during my youth.

Wright

It sounds as if to me she wasn't all that disabled on the bottomline.

Garvey

There's a lot to be said for someone who has determination and heart and will power. She was obviously limited in what she could do, but she found ways of accomplishing her tasks. It was difficult for her to cook because of the difficulty she had with moving hot pans and cooking utensils, but she would. She would also teach me how to cook and by the time I went to college I was a pretty good cook. My dates were impressed when I'd have them over for Sunday afternoon meals.

Wright

So what was your toughest setback growing up—perhaps in high school or in college—and what did it teach you that may have impacted your success as an adult?

Garvey

I would have to say the first biggest setback in my life was in 1970. I had signed in 1968 and played about a season and a half in the Minor Leagues. Then all of a sudden I won the third base job in the spring of 1970, and I went to Los Angeles—I'm on my way to the Hall of Fame, and taking the Dodgers to the World Championship—and within three weeks, I was down in Triple A. I had batted a .228 in the Majors, I bobbled a few balls and the team wasn't doing very well. I got back to Triple A which was Spokane, Washington. The manager was Tommy Lasorda; he had been my first manager in Ogden in '68.

Tommy greeted me at the airport, and said, "I know you're disappointed and you're probably down and you feel you've let people down." He said, "We're going to start working and get you back to the Major Leagues," and that's what he did.

Every afternoon at 2:00, we'd go out and he'd throw to Bobby Valentine, Bill Buckner and me and he dedicated his life to helping us. Of course, most people who know baseball know Tom and his commitment to the game, but he dedicated his life to making us Major Leaguers. I believe that year, that team was voted the greatest team in Pacific Coast history. We won our Division with twenty-two games and polished Hawaii four straight in the Pacific Coast Championships. I think ten or eleven guys on that team went on to play at least nine years in the Majors, every one of them. It was a fabulous team managed by a man who loved the game and who loved his involvement with young players—he taught us how to be great professionals.

I was introduced to success and then I learned what to do when thrown a curve—a fastball inside—when I went back to Triple A. Then I worked, and worked and worked some more to make myself at least average if not better at my deficiencies. Then I returned to the Majors.

When I went back to the Majors I was a man without a position—I was a third baseman but because I had suffered a shoulder separation playing football in Michigan State in my first year I didn't quite throw the same. I didn't have quite the same strength in my arm, so all of a sudden the wild-armed third baseman isn't desired very much. But playing in the Major Leagues for the Dodgers stayed with me for a while, and then I was put in left field a little bit. In 1973 I was the twenty-fourth or twenty-fifth man on the team and started pinch-hitting in the early or the middle part of the game and started getting hits. All of a sudden by July 23 I was leading the National League in pinch-hitting. Between double headers that day against Cincinnati, Walter Austin came by and said, "Hey kid, you want to play first?"

Looking at him I paused for a second, and said, "Oh, sure!" I had only played one game in Little League and one game in Triple A, but I wasn't going to tell him!

That day I played in the second game of the triple-header. I played first, I didn't trip over the bag and got a couple of doubles and we won the game. After the game Austin said, "Well, kid, you're in there tomorrow and then we're on the road this coming week, so get ready to play some first base." That was the turning point in my career.

Wright

Somebody told me something interesting years ago, I don't even remember where—it could have been in some business meeting or seminar or something, training session, or something I was attending—I never will forget it. He said that if you're walking down a field and see a turtle sitting on a fence post, you could bet he didn't get up there by himself. So I wonder what would have happened if Lasorda hadn't met you when you came back?

Garvey

Oh, I probably would have taken a couple of days to reorganize my thinking—I never was one to really dwell on defeat or setbacks and so forth. I usually took only a short amount of time to do that, which, being human you have to feel sorry for yourself and feel down; but within a day or two you say, "Okay, let's put a new game plan together to accomplish our original goal."

I obviously was helped by Tom Lasorda and the other guys who were there to help pick me up and get me back into the game—the Spokane Indians baseball. I was up and down that season. Then I struggled the next two years as I mentioned, not having a real accurate arm. My offense was developing and then suddenly, in 1973, it all came together and I became a first baseman. I think there are certain destinies a person has in life and that was one of them for me.

I went out and won four Golden Gloves at first base and hit the highest fielding percentage of all time. I set a wave toward short or first baseman with Peat Rose and guys like him.

Wright

When people talk about star athletes, the conversation often turns to commitment and dedication. Only a small minority of athletes ever reach the big leagues because it takes a level of commitment few are willing to make, as I understand it. What kind of commitment did you make, and does commitment play a role in success outside sports?

Garvey

Oh, I think so. I think commitment is important throughout life in whatever we do. I don't think we'll ever truly be successful as individuals, as husbands and wives, as businessmen and women, if we don't take that step towards making the commitment to be the very best we can be in whatever it is.

I know I told that to my older four daughters who went to great colleges. They went to Georgetown, Berkeley, Boulder, and UCLA, and didn't necessarily pursue their major but did other things. They asked me, "Are you disappointed?"

I replied "No." I said, "I just want you to think in terms of being the best in whatever you do—the best obstetrician, the best movie producer, the best investment banker." I told them that in life you will realize eventually, as time goes on, it's not necessarily *what* you do, it's the commitment, the dedication, and the perseverance to your job or task that will make the difference.

What's also important is giving back. People used to say, "Why do you spend so much time with charities?"

It's because I've been so blessed to have the ability to reach the ultimate level—to win World Series and to play All Star games, and to be up on the podium delivering a message—I would be remiss if I didn't state the things that made me successful and that I think will make all people successful if they just concentrate on them and put them down on their list—on their game plan.

What I try to do is take my celebrity—my star status—and deliver it verbally to the people I try to reach, whether it's an audience, or a charity, or a social group, or a medical group, or a religious group.

Wright

Can you think of any specific things you did behind the scenes during your baseball career that helped you succeed—things your fans never knew or thought about and maybe things that were not glamorous or fun—mundane things that gave you an edge on the playing field?

Garvey

I think when you're able to divert popularity, celebrity, stardom, and success to helping others, I think it gives a very deep satisfaction. It punctuates why we're on this earth. Those of us who are Christians and who believe in Jesus Christ and God and the Bible and who believe in giving back in this way, you don't need the headlines, you don't need to be in front of the camera, and you don't need to be on the radio. The things you do out of the spotlight probably give you the most satisfaction. There are times when I've been honored with awards and so forth. I truly appreciated them but probably the times when people didn't see me do something or say something or make a commitment to something were the times that truly touched my heart.

Wright

An example of that is the trouble we had today getting together for this interview because you were at your eleven-year-old son's birthday party. I really understand that!

Garvey

Oh yeah.

Wright

I've got a fifteen-year-old myself, and I would have stayed here all day and waited on you because we take priorities like that seriously.

Garvey

It's just the little extra things you do they don't forget. Both my wife Candace and I spent the morning making the cupcakes look like baseballs. He was a little embarrassed when we brought them out with his friends there and all, but he's not going to forget it, and that's what this is all about. We can be there for the good times and we're always going to be there when our kids are sick or needy, but it's those little things like birthdays or graduations that are so important—the pictures are everlasting.

Wright

Yeah, I hope my daughter remembers the times I when I made it because I certainly remember the times when my dad didn't.

Garvey

Yeah, you're right, that's the irony. You remember the don'ts probably more than the do's until you get older and then you're a father or a mother or a grandfather or a grandmother. It's just growing and maturing in life—it takes some years. You held it against your parents because they weren't there sometimes and then you think of the times they were there, and you remember that was great. That's what I want to do. As parents we set that example so our kids can do the same—be there—for their kids.

Wright

After I got to be a man, I cut my dad some slack.

Garvey

Sounds right, yeah.

Wright

I knew how hard it was for him—he worked hard.

Garvey

We don't really realize that fact about our parents. When I travel a lot, the kids realize in a way that Daddy is out working, but they don't really understand. I would come home and get up at 5:00 in the morning and probably won't be home until 9:00 or 10:00 P.M. If I didn't have children I'd have probably gotten up at 7:30 or 8:00, have breakfast and then catch the 11:00 P.M. or 12:00 A.M. to come home. Every time I get up early like that, though, I'm coming home because there's a soccer practice or a baseball practice or a recital or whatever. That's the fine print of the parenting contract.

Wright

Oh yeah!

Garvey

We don't always read the fine print.

Wright

Let's talk about one of your biggest games and see if we can draw some correlations between clutch hitting and peak performance in business. Looking back on your career, is there one particular time at bat that comes to mind when you think of coming through in the clutch, and could you tell us about it?

Garvey

I have several of them. I measure my accomplishments on how they influence people—effect people. The home run against the Cubs off of Lee Smith in the fourth game of the playoffs in 1984 probably had the greatest effect on people—the Padre fans—they hadn't won before. It was that home run in the bottom of the ninth—the game that got us into the final fifth game in that playoff—was when the fans suddenly realized, "Hey, you know, we can win! This is a team that can win. This is a team that can come from behind. This is a team that doesn't give up. We're not going to give up. We're going to be there tomorrow."

People come up to me today and tell me where they were when I hit the home run that night; some of them had been at the stadium.

Wright

You might be on the Mayflower.

Garvey

In Los Angeles I hit home runs—we went to four World Series there—and the World Championship in '81; but the Padre homerun really convinced fans who were skeptics that the team could win and they could become winners. That was the beginning of Padre history per se.

Wright

So you're saying you have to see it in your mind before you actually see it?

Garvey

Well, visualization is important. There are people who can visualize and can dream, and then there are others who are skeptics—who have to be shown. I think there are a lot of optimistic people who believed we were going to win but there were also a lot of skeptics who were saying to themselves, "Ah, they haven't won—in what way are they going to lose tonight?" Then, when we hit the homeruns, it surprised them. We came from line one—we beat the Cubs! Everybody was expecting the Cubs to beat *us*. Once we did that they became believers.

The next day 60,000 people—it sounded like 250,000—were there for us. I think they were a significant reason why we won the next day because we were down three to nothing in the fifth. One thing led to another and all of a sudden Gossage had the ball with two outs and two strikes in the bottom of the ninth. We polished them off and we went to the World Series.

Wright

Well, you're a legend as a real clutch performer, Steve, someone who plays their best when the stakes are the highest. Some people in sports and business have a hard time coming through under pressure. In fact, I can think of a few business meetings in which I choked. Do you have any advice for our readers that might help them "hit the ball out of the park" when it really counts the most?

Garvey

I think the most important thing is preparation and then knowing what the game is that day—knowing who the opposition is, doing your research, finding out who they are, what they're trying to accomplish—then doing your own homework as to what you're going to present or what you're trying to sell. Then go in there without a fear of failure—I think that's the most important thing.

I think many times people go in fearing that they're not going to be successful—they're going to fail, they're going to make a mistake. That's why I always wanted to be up with the bases loaded and two out in the ninth and down by a run. I wanted the chance to be the hero. If I failed, then I failed "daringly" as they say—I failed swinging.

Go out there swinging. We're all human, we're fallible, we make mistakes; but if we prepare, and we know the opposition, if we go out and we make the best pitch we can, then it's out of our hands at the time. If no matter what you say you're not going to win the account or make the sale, you should feel good about the effort you made.

That's why I've always appreciated the Special Olympics and what they do. In the Special Olympics it's not about winning or losing—it's about participating, it's about putting out the best effort you can. They inspire me to keep pitching at all times.

Wright

You know in life and business, transition is hard for many people. In our business culture, men and women are often forced to change jobs or even professions more than once in their lifetime. Was there a transition like that for you when you retired from professional baseball? Are there some lessons our readers can take away from that transition?

Garvey

We're creatures of habit. I think we get very comfortable with doing what we do especially if we develop this high level of skill for it. But I started planning for what we term "after the cheering stops"—for life after baseball. I had started a marketing company and I had worked for Pepsi Cola, and Adidas, and a number of other companies to get a sense of business—on the job training. Then when the time came, I already had Garvey Marketing Group up and running, and was still working at other companies and corporations, continuing to get an understanding of business and develop my skills.

It goes back to what we talked about before—planning. It's important to have a year plan, a three-year plan, and a five-year plan. You have to keep assessing where you are in your own business and your own industry. You have to ask yourself if you like what you do. If you don't like what you do, it can be very, very difficult and very stressful. You have to decide if you want to change your lifestyle and do something that will allow yourself to enjoy your work better and try to be more successful and more productive at it, but might not make as much money. Often that equates to longevity—more enthusiasm for work and more dedication—you're not affected by the nuances of not enjoying what you do.

Wright

Steve, it's been an absolute pleasure visiting with you today, but before we go, can you tell us how you spend your time these days? Do you have any final words of wisdom for our readers?

Garvey

My biggest job nowadays is keeping track of five daughters and two sons!

Wright

I hear that!

Garvey

I have a wonderful wife who's gone through about five years of difficult times with degenerative back disease. She had an operation last December and an eight-month healing process. She's doing very well but the doctor said she can't bend, lift, or twist, and we've tried to figure out what's left! But she's doing very, very well. So, I'm busy with that and with Garvey Media Group, which is a media consulting company I created when I made the transition from marketing and communications into media consulting.

Speaking is very important to me. I probably do forty to forty-five corporate speeches a year, and tailor those speeches to the needs of the client. As I always say when I first get on the platform, "Instead of trying to hit a homerun at the bottom of the ninth now, my goal is to put my heart and soul into saying something of benefit to your mind and body in an hour." It's quite a challenge, but I love that.

When I finish a speech, I always try to end it by saying, "When we come into this world we bring nothing with us, and when we leave, we take nothing with us; but if we can make it a better place while we're here, then we've been a winner in God's eyes." I usually get a pretty nice response from that. I think people understand we all struggle and we're faced with families and jobs and trying to be the best we can be and it's tough; but if we keep making the effort every day then I think we'll be successful.

Wright

In making decisions in your life today, is faith important to you?

Garvey

Very, very important. I started by my being baptized and confirmed as a Catholic back in 1963, I think. I'd go to Mass before a football game in the fall and it became really the foundation of my life. I don't think I have the right to preach, but I think I have the right to speak at the podium and to mention that I am a Christian and that I do have faith; that it's been a strong part of my life and my family's life. I encourage others to explore it in whatever direction or whatever it happens to be for them. It's interesting that when I'm done there are always half a dozen or a dozen people who come up and say, "I heard you clearly." It's great.

Wright

Well, today we have been talking with "Mr. Dodger"—Steve Garvey. Steve, thanks a lot for taking time with us for our book, *The Game Matters.*

Garvey

Oh, it was a pleasure. Thanks.

About The Author

Steve Garvey is a ten-time MLB All-Star and a four-time Gold Glove winner. He holds the record for the highest career fielding percentage by a first baseman and is the only player in the history of baseball to have an errorless season at first base. Garvey was named as the National League MVP in 1974, the All-Star Game MVP in 1974 and 1978, Playoff MVP in 1974, 1977 and 1984 and on April 18, 1988 his #6 was retired by the San Diego Padres. To only focus on Steve Garvey's baseball accomplishments would leave out a lifetime of achievements as a businessman, philanthropist, volunteer and most importantly a devoted family man. As a father of seven children Garvey understands that in the ever-changing world we live in there is a great necessity of being a man of honor, integrity and quality.

Steve Garvey
NOPA Sports
c/o: Steve Garvey
1806 Watermere Lane
Windermere, FL 34786
Phone: 888.550.6672
Fax: 407.445.7180
Email: info@stevegarvey.com
www.stevegarvey.com

Chapter Two

DOUG HANSON

THE INTERVIEW

David E. Wright (Wright)

Today we're talking to Doug Hanson. Doug was born and raised in a small town in Texas where he developed a humble spirit to go along with his down-to-earth approach to life. Although he has impacted thousands of people's lives through his seminars and books, when asked about his success, Doug insists that *he* is the one who has been blessed.

Doug has a broad range of skills and has enjoyed impressive accomplishments in athletics, business, music, and pubic speaking. In his presentations, Doug moves people with a witty, hilarious storytelling style that holds his audience captivated. He was a featured facilitator and speaker for seven consecutive years at Tony Robbins famous Life Mastery University seminar in Hawaii, and Doug has shared the stage with such notable figures as George Bush, Roger Clemens (the Major League Baseball Hall of Famer), and Rudy Ruettiger, (Notre Dame football hero who's story became a Hollywood movie).

Doug was also selected by the NFL Super Bowl host committee to train the 6,000 volunteers and 200 captains who represented Houston at the 2004 Super Bowl. Doug has a variety of topics and programs and is repeatedly brought back by his clients as a speaker and consultant for follow-up keynote addresses, training sessions, and ongoing organizational development.

Doug, welcome to *The Game Matters.*

Doug Hanson (Hanson)

Thank you, I'm very excited and honored to be here.

Wright

Each year you motivate thousands of people in your seminars, yet you don't refer to yourself as a motivational speaker, so what's up with that?

Hanson

Well, I think motivation is very important, but it won't solve your problems. I tell people all the time, if you're dead broke, it doesn't do much good to close your eyes and put your hands in your pockets, put a big smile on your face and just start repeating to yourself, "I'm loaded with cash, I'm loaded with cash," because when you open your eyes, you're still broke!

Now, don't get me wrong. I'm a huge fan of motivation, but I think people misunderstand it, and therefore, misuse it. Motivation isn't the solution, it's what gives you the energy and wherewithal to find and act on the solution. I always say motivation is like a warm bath, you need it every day. If you don't take a bath every day, what will happen to you? You'll begin to stink! People will begin to avoid you. Some people will come to you and say, "Hey buddy, you stink!" If you don't get a little motivation every day, I think the same thing will happen to your attitude. Your disposition on life will begin to stink and people will begin to avoid you. Some will describe you as negative, cranky, or moody, which is another way of saying, "You stink." Pretty soon we'll get a sour outlook on life, and we all know that our repetitive thoughts are the key to directing our results.

I think people come to the wrong conclusion about motivation when they see film clips of coaches motivating their players in the locker room—they think the motivation alone is what wins the game. People translate that into their life and think, "If I can just get pumped up enough, I'll succeed," and they try to shortcut the building blocks of success—the fundamentals: the repetitions, the hard work, and the perseverance.

Wright

So, what do you call yourself?

Hanson

Well, I gave myself a new title awhile back, it's one that incorporates motivation, but also much more. My new title is directed by my experiences in athletics. I call myself a "Transformation Coach." I love this title for three main reasons:

The first reason focuses on the word "transformation." I've always loved sports. I love playing and I love watching. I love everything about sports and I think there is no better way to prepare a young person for life than through sports. It's all there: setting goals, discipline, hard work, hot streaks, cold streaks, dealing with pressure, celebration, and teamwork. And you can't be a sportsman without recognizing the differences a coach makes.

I love to watch how different coaches work—their strategies, their style, and how they handle different players, how they teach their philosophies and so forth. Every team has a different culture and I think the head coach creates it. Good coaches make a lasting change in their players. They "Transform" them into better *people,* not just better players. I've talked to players who've played for great coaches and they always have a story about how that coach helped shape their life. They weren't just motivated; they were influenced to be a different person—a better person. Instead of being a speaker who just motivates people, I want to help transform lives for the better, so I gave myself this new title as Transformation Coach. This title helps me to remember that my objective is more than just motivation; it's to help my audiences transform the way they think. Because, I believe if you change the way someone thinks, you change everything. Motivation is important, but it's temporary. Transformations are for life!

The second reason I like this title is a simple one. I think we tend to make things harder in our mind than they are in reality. For example, I always wanted to be a coach, so by declaring this title for myself, I now am a coach! Isn't that simple? This is my playful way of saying to people, "just do it."

We are usually looking for reasons why we can't do something instead of why we can. I always wanted to be a coach but I always talked myself out of it for a variety of reasons from things like, the income level of the coaching profession, or the experience needed that I didn't have, or how difficult it would be to get started, etc. Sometimes all we have to do is just decide what we want to do and *voila*—there it is!

I'll give you a real world example: When I meet people on the plane, to my surprise they are usually very impressed that I'm a motivational speaker. They always ask, "How do you become a speaker?" like it's some really difficult process, or a test you have to pass. I always say, in a joking way, "If you really want to be a speaker, here's what you do: first, you go to Office Depot." They usually giggle at this point. Then I add, "Have them print some business cards with your name on the front and "motivational speaker" as the title underneath. There, you're done. Now all you do is go to your next party, hand them out to everyone, and then fake it 'til you make it." They always laugh and I laugh along with them. Then I change my tone of voice to a more serious one and say to them, "Really! That's all there is to it."

I've found that most people have something inside of them that they desperately want to do but they keep making it harder than it should be. Maybe it's writing a book, or learning to play an instrument, speaking a foreign language, or maybe becoming a gourmet cook or even becoming a coach. They just make it harder than it has to be. So, by simply claiming this title of "Transformation Coach" is my way of saying to everyone, "If you want to do something, just do it. Don't make it harder than it is."

The *main* reason I like the title Transformation Coach is because I believe we are *all* transformation coaches. I've always thought of myself as a coach primarily because I am one of the two coaches in my family—my wife being the other one. Just like a sports coach does with his team, my wife and I establish the culture in our family. We strategize together our goals for each other and our kids. We establish the rules and we hold each other and the kids accountable. We celebrate together and we struggle together. I think the family is the ultimate team and parents are the ultimate coaches.

You see, as a speaker, I want to connect with my audience. I don't want them to see me as someone who's up on stage, larger than life. If they could step into my shoes they would see that I'm no different than they are. I have the same doubts, fears, problems, setbacks, and all the other challenges of life. But according to studies, the number one fear for people in this world is the thought of speaking in public. The same study reveals that the fear of death is number four on the list. Now, I have to admit, I don't buy it. I have to think that if I put someone on stage and held a gun to their head and said, "Give us a speech or I'll shoot," I just don't believe they would surrender to the situation and scream, "Go ahead, pull the trigger, I'm not going to say a word!"

Regardless, the point is that most people don't see themselves as ever being able to get up on stage and give a motivational speech. So the title "Motivational Speaker" could actually separate me from my audience. What speaker would want that? I would never want my audience to think I am different than they are. So I want a title everyone can relate to, one that helps each member of my audience realize that we're all the same and we're all in the game of life together. Transformation Coach is perfect. Every person on the planet is a transformation coach.

Wright

What exactly does it mean to be a Transformation Coach?

Hanson

First, we all have to transform our own lives and our own thoughts on a daily basis. When tough times hit we have to be able to pick ourselves up by the bootstraps and get going again. I always say, "It takes courage to be happy." Anyone can be unhappy, it takes no effort or courage at all to be unhappy, but happy people are courageous. Happy people are also students of transformation. They've learned how to find the good in all situations in their life.

Most people are waiting for happiness in their lives. They think it's something that will happen to them when they reach a certain place in their life or if they acquire certain things. I hear people say, "If I just had more money, then I'd be happy." When I hear that I always say, "You've got the formula backwards." I tell them, "If you'll find a way to be happy, then you'll have more money."

I sometimes hear people say, "If I could just meet that man or that woman of my dreams, then I'd be happy." Once again I tell them, "If you'll get happy, you'll meet the man or woman of your dreams." So, in order to find happiness and success in life, we must spend less time trying to avoid life's challenges and more time learning how to transform our mindset and approach toward them.

Second, we all transform other people around us. Think about what a mom or a dad does when their six-year-old son comes home from a rotten day at school—a day where his favorite teacher scolded them for misbehaving, the school bully pushed him down at recess and everyone laughed at him, and then on the bus ride home he realizes he left some homework in his desk which means he's sure to get in trouble again tomorrow—one of those days where everything is going wrong and the child comes home with tears in his eyes. What does the mom do when she sees her son in such a sad state and hears of his rotten day? Does she say, "Hey, you're bringing me down here, deal with it, I've got problems of my own"? Of course not. No matter what has happened in her day, she's fully present for her son. She gets on her knees and embraces the child with a comforting hug that only mom or dad can give. Then her mind begins to race, searching for anything that will cheer her son up. She thinks of her childhood and tells him a story of how she went through similar situations and then she tells him how it all worked out. In other words, she gave her son hope that everything would turn out okay. That's a transformation. She didn't fix the world, or all the problems the child experienced, but she did help him see the world and those problems differently. That's a transformation.

We're all in the transformation business, ourselves first, then those around us. So, it's my hope that after someone attends one of my seminars, they see themselves as a transformation coach too. And I hope they take their new title very seriously.

Wright

Well, you've obviously done a pretty good job of transforming your own life. You've been successful in sports and business. You have a beautiful family, a wife of twenty years, and you get hundreds of letters each year from business leaders and individuals who've attended your live seminars thanking you for transforming their company and their personal lives as well. So, what's your secret?

Hanson

I'm not sure I have a secret but I do have a concept I learned from my years as a player, coach, and fan of competitive athletics. In order to better grasp this idea, let me ask you a question: Don't you find it interesting that the team with the most talent doesn't always win? I've always been fascinated by this. Why is that? Shouldn't the team with the most talent win every time? Here's another interesting phenomenon: once a team starts a winning tradition, isn't it amazing how that program continues to thrive while teams who constantly lose seem to struggle year after year, regardless of how much new talent they acquire during the off-season?

Over the years as a player, coach, and businessperson, I've learned something that sheds light on these observations. Like most athletes

I learned first hand the benefits of discipline, fundamentals, hard work, setting goals, and perseverance. More than anything, however, I learned that winning programs have a process they never waiver from, and that process creates their winner's mindset. Winning coaches don't walk out on the practice field and say, "What should we work on today?" They have every minute of every practice well thought out in advance. They have a road map for success and they follow it to the letter. Sometimes people think these coaches are crazy. For example, John Wooden would begin every year by giving his players a lesson on how to put on their socks properly. He believed this simple fundamental concept would eliminate unnecessary blisters, pain, and medical treatments and would therefore increase the effectiveness of his practice sessions and the players' concentration. Before you make fun of this concept you should know that Coach Wooden won ten national championships in twelve years. No other college basketball coach has ever won more than four national championships in an entire lifetime. Coach Wooden won ten in twelve years!

Coach Vince Lombardi, the legendary coach of the Green Bay Packers would start off each season by holding up a football and saying, "Gentlemen, this is a football." He would then make sure they understood the basic concepts of the game. Each year his first few weeks of practices were focused on the basics of blocking and tackling, footwork, and body position. He would drive home the basics until his players could do them in their sleep. He didn't let anyone get sidetracked with trick plays or fancy formations until everyone understood the basics.

Years ago I became captivated with understanding the basics that make a sports team successful. I found that every coach has many different things that they believe are important but they also had some things in common. I was able to identify a five-step process that they all did one way or another, whether they knew it or not. I then began to interview successful businessmen and women and found that the process had been applied in their life as well.

I began to apply it in my life. The results have been staggering for me. Yes, my finances skyrocketed but I hope people understand that I don't believe my finances improved because of a magic formula. Instead, I feel the process helped me to be happy and eager to enjoy every day to the fullest. There's something about having a plan that is uplifting and freeing. An experienced baker doesn't worry if the bread will rise—he knows it will. He's followed the plan that has worked a thousand times before and has been working for generations before him. He doesn't worry about it. He follows the plan and then lets the bread rise "when it's time." He doesn't try to rush it because he knows that won't work.

Having a plan for my life allowed me to be free from stress and just be myself. It gave me a peace of mind that allowed me to be a better husband, father, friend, and co-worker. Before long, opportunities were coming to me that I could have never imagined, and yes, my finances improved dramatically. The best part, however, is that I truly enjoy my life, my wife, my children, all the other people in and aspects of my life. So often I see people who are successful on the surface, but they're literally dying inside from stress, worry, and guilt for not being the kind of spouse or parent they think they should be.

Once you have a plan, you can then simply work the plan and let everything happen as God intended.

Wright

Well, you've sold me! Can you share your success process with us?

Hanson

Absolutely. Sharing this process has become my passion. I call it "Meta-More-Phosis." Obviously, the word metamorphosis itself is in alignment with my self-proclaimed title of "Transformation Coach," something we discussed in detail earlier. The key to the Meta-More-Phosis system is the word in the middle: "More." (I had to modify the actual spelling a bit to meet my needs since there is not an "e" in the word metamorphosis following the first three letters "Mor".) This model is built on the premise that nothing on this planet is in a static state. Everything is ever changing. Everything is either thriving or dying, growing or eroding. The five-step Meta-More-Phosis process capitalizes on the concept of constant improvement and growth, i.e.—More!

The five steps include:

1. Expect More – Raise Your Standards
2. Become More – Take Personal Responsibility
3. Feel More – Get Passionate – Play Full Out
4. Think More – Have A Plan and Keep Improving It
5. Do More – Take Action

Now, before I begin explaining these five steps I must give a word of caution. I think all too often people are linking their self-worth and their happiness to how much "stuff" they have. This is not the concept of "More" I'm referring to in the model. I don't believe there is anything wrong with setting goals to have more money, or more toys, or more material things, but in order for the Meta-More-Phosis model to work, you must first begin from a place of true appreciation for what you already have. I could fill the rest of this book on the subject of appreciation alone. It is a subject I'm very passionate about. I think it is one of the cornerstones of happiness and having a fulfilled life.

So often people think they will be happy if they only had "more" of something (usually money) when all they need to be happy is simply to take inventory of what they already have. We all know someone who "has everything" according to the world's standards. They have the house, the car, the beautiful wife, the talented kids, tons of money and everything else we all think would bring us happiness, and yet those people are the most miserable, bitter, unhappy people on the earth.

We also know someone who has nothing by the world's standards. They have a run-down house, an old beat-up car, no luxuries, and live paycheck to paycheck, but every time we see them they have a smile on their face. These examples prove that it's not more stuff that makes you happy. Becoming the kind of person who can attract a better lifestyle and helping others along the way is what really makes you happy.

This Meta-More-Phosis model is designed for mentally mature people, people who are thinkers and who are committed to improving every day—people who understand that "more" in this context is about becoming the kind of person who wants to attract abundance in their life such as, joy, fulfillment, and love, not just "more" material possessions. There's nothing wrong with wanting to be a millionaire. The problem, however, can be in your reason *why* you want to be a millionaire. I always say I want to be a millionaire because I want to *become* the kind of person who can attract a million dollars, not because I want to buy a million dollars worth of stuff or have a million dollars worth of power. People who can attract a million dollars usually add lots of value to their community. They usually make a difference in people's lives. And even though they already think like a millionaire, they want to keep improving. They'll even invite a billionaire over every now and then for advice on how they can do better! Which leads to the first step in the model: Expect More.

Wright

I'm guessing, expect more is about setting goals and establishing a clear vision, is that correct?

Hanson

Yes it is. But it's also about "raising your standards," with one important distinction. I think most everyone understands the concept of setting goals and even understand the benefits of doing so, but yet they still struggle with sitting down and doing it. Most people can't remember the last time they sat down and put their desires and goals in life in writing. Have you ever wondered why? After all, we know the benefits of written goals, why don't we do it? You see, most people have never been taught about the conflict that is going on inside their mind on a daily basis. This conflict is what stops us from writing everything down and being fully committed. Once you understand this conflict, your ability to set goals and achieve them is dramatically improved. I call it "the Dance of the Spirit and the Flesh."

We all have one thing in common when it comes to our brain. We all have an area in our brain that is completely focused on one thing—*survival!* We don't have to be taught to survive, it's built into our instincts much like a squirrel never has to be taught to gather nuts in the spring or a migratory bird never has to be taught to fly south for winter. It is hard-wired into the primitive part of their brains. Sometimes this is referred to as the "reptilian brain" or the "first brain." This basic need to survive is what has kept us alive as a species all these years and is something we have in common with all other living mammals on the planet. This part of our brain is constantly seeking safety, security, and comfort. It is always on the lookout for danger and can therefore cause us to always live in fear. However, humans also have a more developed part of the brain. This part of our brain is highly evolved and is what separates us from lower species. It's called the "neocortex" and it processes rational thoughts. The neocortex is what allows us to dream, solve problems, and perform amazing feats of creation and conceptual thinking. It is the part of our brain that lets us talk to ourselves and visualize something better than what currently exists. When the primitive, reptilian brain says, "This could be dangerous!" it's our neocortex that steps in and says, "Calm down. Everything is okay." Some people say this is where our spirit actually resides, the part of us that lives after our physical body is dead. Thus we have a conflict. The primitive side of the brain is always seeking comfort for the body, whereas the higher functioning part of the brain (where your spirit resides), is always seeking fuller expression. The spirit is saying to you, "Let's do more, be more, have more, and experience more in this short time we have on earth." But the primitive side is saying, "Are you crazy? We could be hurt. It will be a lot of work. You've never done anything like that before. You should just stay where you are and safely live out the rest of your life." That's why I call this the dance of the Spirit and the Flesh. What we need to do is learn to let our Spirit take the lead! When people dream, it's scary! I mean, if you really had the skills to do more with your life, wouldn't you already be doing it? So the very concept of setting a goal to do more or be more than you already are causes your reptilian brain to say, "You can't do it." So, we let the dream die and move back to more "achievable" endeavors. We settle for less, not "more," and we simply survive.

This is the point where the mature person—one who is at a higher level of awareness—lets his spirit take the lead in the dance of the spirit and the flesh. He begins to focus on all the reasons he *can* do it. He recognizes his fears and rationalizes why he can succeed. Then he visualizes what his life will be like when he takes action and makes it all come true. He says things to himself like, "I have a process that works," and, "I have a plan of action," and, "I wasn't a mistake," and "God has big plans for me and I have faith in His timing for all things." The fears are still there, protecting him when necessary, but they don't take the lead in the dance. The spirit leads the dance in a winner's heart.

I remember when I was in high school football. I was a ninety-pound weakling in my freshman year and I went out for football. I hold the distinction as being the first guy in the history of my high school who was turned away. It wasn't because the coaches didn't like me, it was just the opposite—they loved me. They were close friends with my parents and they didn't want me to get hurt, so they asked me to sit out a year. I came back my next year; I weighed ninety-four pounds and they let me play. I still haven't figured that one out. Regardless, I didn't play a single down in a game that year. Everyone referred to me as "Little Doug," and that was my personal identity as well.

Just before my senior year came around, our head coach was promoted to athletic director and his staff moved on to other schools. A new head coach was brought in with an entirely new coaching staff. None of these new leaders knew me as "Little Doug." I had actually started getting a little bigger and faster but I hadn't realized it, and neither had anyone else. I never saw myself as a great athlete so I was living up to my own expectations. After a few months of testing and practices, the new head coach approached me and said, "Doug you're one of our best athletes. I 'expect' big things from you next year."

I remember thinking, "Man, we're in for a long year!"

He continued, "I want you to be a leader next year, and I want you to help take this team to new places."

That year I was named All District First Team on offense and Second Team All District on defense. My name was in the paper several times and people recognized me in my community as a hard worker who wouldn't quit. My whole life from that year on was totally different. I went on to play college football and even went to two NFL tryouts.

This is what coaches do; that's why I like the title, Transformation Coach. They raise our standards, which is the concept here. They expect more from us and believe in us more than we do ourselves. They raise our standards to take us to levels we never thought we could achieve. They challenge our beliefs and help us get a clearer vision. As a personal Transformation Coach, each of us need to get a clear picture of what we want in our life and *expect more* from ourselves each day. Once we master this in our own lives, we gain the respect from others, which will enable us to influence them as well.

Wright

This is great information. Now I understand why setting goals and "Expecting More" is so important, and so difficult. What is step number 2 in the Meta-More-Phosis?

Hanson

The second step is "Become More," which is another way of saying, take personal responsibility for your life. It's so easy to blame the world, the economy, and the government, or whatever else you want to blame—your wife, your kids, or your boss. Great people recognize that the world isn't always fair so they quit blaming everyone and move on.

An important starting point to begin the process of taking responsibility and "Becoming More" is by managing your *state of mind.* I always say there are two kinds of people: There are those people who brighten the room when they walk in, and those who brighten it when they leave. After I explain this philosophy to my audiences I always ask, "Which one are you? Do people refer to you as someone who brightens a room when you walk in?" Be honest with yourself. If you're someone who brightens the room when you leave, it's okay, because you can fix that starting right now! You can make the decision this instant to start being a happier, kinder person. This one change in your approach will dramatically change your life: to be the kind of person who builds up other people, who is positive, who has kind things to say, who sees the world as a good place, and who is looking to make a difference in the world. That's one area that you can take responsibility and Become More.

We can also take responsibility for how we react to adversity. Everyone knows that adversity is a prerequisite for growth and happiness, but people are often more focused on avoiding adversity than on recognizing that something good will always come from it. As Napoleon Hill said in his timeless book, *Think and Grow Rich,* "Every adversity carries with it the seed for equal or greater benefit."

Have you ever looked back on a time that you once considered to be the worst time of your life and later said, "Wow, that was the best thing that ever happened to me"? We all have. What if we started giving thanks in advance? Try it. At the end of this paragraph, stop reading this book for a moment and think of a challenge you are facing right now—something that's had you worried, or stressed, or even depressed. Now think of all the good things that "could" come from this adversity over time and give thanks for it in advance. Go ahead and do this little exercise now.

How did that feel? This little discipline in the area of personal responsibility—"Becoming More"—will take you from being a victim to being fully engaged when forced to face life's challenges.

Another discipline that truly successful people understand about "Becoming More" is that we must keep improving. Successful people don't wish for easier challenges, they long for more skills. They know that one of the keys to happiness and success is constant and never-ending improvement. The Japanese have a single word this concept:

Kaizen. People who understand this philosophy read good books, they journal their life and their thoughts, and they never stop learning. They also associate with good people. This is one of my favorites. Becoming More is directly linked to associating with good people—quality people. I'm not saying turn your back on people who aren't successful or who are down on their luck. We all need to have compassion for one another and help each other. What I *am* saying, however, is to make a conscious effort to surround yourself with people who are committed to learning, who help others, who take the high road when it comes to matters of integrity, and who will hold you accountable in your journey through life.

You don't have to always know these people personally. You can associate with them through their books, their speeches, or if available, through their audio CDs. Dreyton McClain, the owner of the Houston Astros, is a good example for me. Although I don't know Mr. McClain personally, I live in the Houston area so I'm familiar with his leadership style from various interviews I've seen. I was speaking at an event one time where we shared the stage. During his speech he talked about his values and I made notes in my journal that continue to influence me today.

He said the most important advice he'd ever received in his life was from his mother. She would constantly remind him about the importance of whom he associated with. She said, "Your friends' values, character, and behavior will ultimately, to some degree influence who you are." He said every time he came home from college, his mom would hug him and then immediately ask him to sit down and tell her about his friends. He said, "I had to answer her because she wouldn't feed me until I told her everything."

When he was thinking about buying the Houston Astros he asked his mother what she thought. Her reply was, "Tell me about the people you'll be associated with if you buy them." On her last day of life, as she lay on her deathbed in the hospital, she asked him one last time to tell her about his friends and business associates. It was obviously very important to her and I think most would agree that her son turned out pretty well.

Wright

Wow, what a great story. I think I'm beginning to get it. Expecting more opens our minds to possibility and becoming more inspires us to develop ourselves into someone capable and worthy of our goals. So, how does the third step, Feel More, come into play?

Hanson

Well, "Feel More" is all about passion. About playing "Full Out." I coach Roger Clemens' son, Kacy, on my select youth baseball team. In addition to many other records, including the all time strikeout leader, Roger Clemens is a seven-time Cy-Young winner, pro baseball's top honor for a pitcher. He's an intense competitor who knows a little about hard work and success.

Our youth baseball team has been very successful as well and we play all over the country. Because of this, I've had the opportunity to sit with Roger several times and talk to him about sports and life. I don't think anyone would question Roger's commitment to excellence, or his intensity, or his desire to be a champion. His presence alone in the 2004 season—his first year with the Houston Astros—transformed the team into a legitimate World Series contender. For those who don't remember, the Astros were one game away from being in the World Series, with a three game to two lead over the St. Louis Cardinals in a best out of seven series. I don't think it is a coincidence that Roger's first year with the team was the franchise's best year in more than twenty years.

I remember in one of our conversations, he said something to me that had such an impact; I literally got up immediately after he said it and ran to my journal so I could capture it word for word. I think it applies to business people and parents as well. He said, "It has always amazed me that corporate professionals usually put such little value on the emotional side of success. Every athlete I know values the mental or emotional edge as much as they do an advantage in skill." I couldn't agree with him more. The concept of "Feeling More" is really important. As I said earlier, the team with the most talent doesn't always win. It's usually the team that *yearns more,* not simply wants to earn more. If you yearn more for something, you'll play full out to get it. You'll feel the joy of success and the pain of failure in advance. You'll feel these things before they happen and then you'll let those feelings take you farther than your talent will alone. So after you set your goals (Expect More) and take responsibility for your results (Become More), get clear on *why* you need to succeed, (Feel More). What's your compelling "why"? If you want something bad enough, you'll always find a way.

Wright

You're right, people who are passionate do have a clear advantage and they're always more fun to associate with, but wouldn't you agree that Expecting More, Becoming More and Feeling More are focused on the emotional side of success? Don't you have to have tangible activity as well?

Hanson

Yes, that's a great point, and a perfect introduction to the fourth step in of the Meta-More-Phosis process which is “Think More.” I think everyone will agree that a person’s level of thinking is an absolute identifier of what they are going to get in life. I tell people in my seminars all the time, "The results you're getting in your life right now are nothing more than a physical manifestation of your level of consistent thinking.” So, in other words, you become what you think about. There's really no way to sugarcoat this timeless principal, so here it is: If you make three dollars an hour, here's why—you think like a person who makes three dollars an hour, and therefore you manifest an environment that will lead you to three dollars per hour. It's not the government, it's not the economy, it's not taxes or your education level or the type of parents you had, it's you and your level of thinking.

Donald Trump, for example, is on a completely different level of thinking than I am, which is why he has a completely different kind of life, both good and bad. He has considerably more money than I do because he thinks like a person who has more money—he is wiser in the ways of money. He's much more knowledgeable about money than I am, therefore he capitalizes on that knowledge and invests it in a way that I would never dream of.

On the other hand, I have been happily married to the same woman for over twenty years, because I think like a person who values and nurtures lifelong relationships. So, if I want to improve my financial situation, all I need to do is improve my level of thinking in that area. I need to read Trump’s books or other financially successful businessmen’s books. Likewise, if Trump wants to make his most recent marriage work, he's going to have to think a little differently than he has in the past. Who knows, maybe he'll give me a call one day and ask for some advice! As my kids always say, “It could happen”.

A big part of the thinking process is to create a good plan. You have to have a good plan or you're wasting your time. I once heard Tony Robbins say, "If you're headed east looking for a sunset, you need to improve your strategy.” All the vision in the world (Expect More), and all the personal development in the world (Become More), combined with all the passion in the world (Feel More), won't compensate for a flawed plan. You have to have a good plan and you have to keep improving it as things change. We must constantly be thinking about what we're doing and what's working so we can adjust along the way. Sometimes these plans can be simple.

You mentioned Rudy Ruettiger in my introduction. I've spoken at three different events with Rudy so he and I have had a chance to sit and talk. You may recall he had a movie made about his life story and his dream to play football at Notre Dame. Here's this little guy—a nobody by his own description with no money, no connections, and no real athletic achievements per se, who worked in the steel mills—and one day decided he would go back to school—to Notre Dame no less—and play football. He was a long shot by any standard, both academically and as an athlete; but he succeeded. I asked him once if he had a plan and he answered that he did. He said his plan was simple and included five steps:

1. His first objective was to find a way to get around the players and the coaches, so he got on the maintenance crew that mowed the grass at the football fields.
2. Then he said he knew he needed to develop relationships with the people who could influence his future. Since he was around the team and coaching staff while on the maintenance crew, he always looked for ways to help out anyone he could. His plan worked. Over time more and more people knew him by name and they grew to like him.
3. Step three was very difficult but clearly stated—"get a gold helmet"—get on the team and into the locker room. Through his newfound relationships, he found a way to get on the practice team.
4. My favorite is his fourth step. He said step number four was to "get a helmet that fits!" I laughed out loud when he said this. It made me remember times in my life when I had the same attitude. He didn't care initially if everything was perfect, as long as he was going in the right direction. I could imagine him as a young wide-eyed kid getting that first gold helmet and saying to himself, "Who cares if my helmet fits. At least I have a Notre Dame gold helmet! I don't want to cause problems. It's just my

head. I'll be fine. I'll find a way to get a helmet that fits later." He did that and a whole lot more.

5. The fifth and final step was to play in a real Notre Dame football game. For those who don't know the story—here's the littlest guy to ever put on a Notre Dame uniform, who played literally only fifteen seconds in his whole career, made one tackle, and became one of the most famous people who ever graduated from Notre Dame.

The point is that your plans don't always have to be overly sophisticated. Sometimes the best plans are the simplest ones, but you've got to "Think More" and have a plan. A life without a plan is like a ship without a rudder. It only sails in the direction of the current winds and its destination is left to chance. Remember, if you don't have a plan for your life, you'll probably become a part of someone else's plan.

Wright

I can see how this process works. What's the fifth and final step in the Meta-More-Phosis process?

Hanson

I've saved the best for last. It's the one that's probably the most powerful. It's what I call, "Do More." and it's all about taking action. We've all been taught since we were very young that information is power. I disagree. Information is *potential* power. Real power comes from action.

Think about how much information is on the Internet. Everything you could ever want to learn or know is there. The problem is we're drowning in information but starving for wisdom. Information without action is useless. We all know, for example, what kind of food we should eat in order to be healthy, yet we don't do it. We know simple life truths like the benefit of exercise, the power of letting your money compound exponentially over time, and what our spouses need from us to have a happy marriage, yet we don't do what we know we should do. So information is not power, action is.

Real power comes from taking action, and then taking action again, and again, and again. You can't just take action one time and say, "Well, I tried." It's about perseverance. So often people have all the right skills, they have the right support groups, they have everything they need to be successful, but they don't get up off the couch and do it. Of the five steps in the Meta-More-Phosis process, "Do More," is the one that will most separate you from those living a life of mediocrity, or just "getting by." This is especially true if you take creative action.

I remember when I was trying to get into the Executive MBA program at the University of Houston. I wanted to get into the Executive program because their schedule met my work requirements better than the traditional program or night school curriculum. I was twenty-eight years old and was a sales professional in the computer industry. While the night school MBA program took about three and a half to four years to complete, the executive MBA only took a year and a-half and classes were held on weekends, not weekday evenings which would interfere with my business travel and job responsibilities. It wasn't long after I set my goals to be accepted into the executive program that I learned of a few significant obstacles. Number one: they only accepted 60 people per year. Number two: the program cost $20,000 and had to be paid immediately upon acceptance. My wife and I only had about $3,000 in savings at the time. I didn't know exactly how I would raise the money but I knew I would find a way if I could somehow get past the third hurdle—the University of Houston's "age and experience" criteria for acceptance in the program. It stated the students should have fifteen years of business experience and a minimum five to ten years of executive management experience. I was a twenty-eight-year-old salesman with five years of limited business experience. I had never even been a first level manager, much less an executive. So, when I went to apply, the dean in charge of the program told me point blank, "You don't qualify." He didn't even look at my entrance exam test scores, which were more than adequate.

Obviously, I was disappointed. I think most people would have just walked away right then. But I learned through athletics that if you want something bad enough, you have to keep on trying. I asked some friends for advice. One of them enlightened me that alumni have significant clout and influence with their respective universities. I was told if I got enough endorsement letters from previous graduates, the university would probably reconsider. The program was only about ten years old at the time and only about sixty people were accepted each year. That meant I had about 600 possible graduates to work from.

It was 1992 and I was selling computers. Laptop computers were the newest and hottest product in the fast-paced technology industry.

Color laptops were just being introduced at trade shows, but were not available for purchase yet. To have one of your own to showcase to your friends and business associates was a real conversation piece and a sign of success. The company I worked for at the time had recently introduced the very first active matrix color notebook to the market and it was to sell for about $4,500. Being the local sales rep, I had just been assigned five demonstration units to use in my sales efforts.

The day after I was deemed “unqualified” I called the University of Houston Executive MBA offices and pretended I was someone else. I said, “My name is "John Doe" and I'm thinking about applying for your University’s Executive MBA program. I'd like to have a list of recent graduates so I can contact them about their overall experience and impression of the program.” To my surprise they faxed over a list within minutes! Within minutes I realized that five of the recent graduates worked for companies I was already selling computers to. Although I didn’t know these graduates personally, I knew I could utilize my current relationships in their company to professionally and respectfully make contact with them. After my contacts paved the way, I called up those five graduates and said, "My name is Doug Hanson, I work for Toshiba America Information Systems and we have a brand new color laptop that was recently introduced at Comdex (the largest computer trade show at the time). I would like to bring you one to use for a few weeks.” The beauty of this plan was that I was also doing my job. In the process of meeting these people who could help me get into the MBA program, I was developing relationships with important executives and introducing them to our products.

Every customer I called that day enthusiastically accepted my offer and scheduled a time to meet with me. When I delivered their computer, what do you think was hanging on the wall in their office? That’s right, their diploma from the University of Houston Executive MBA program. I would comment on their degree and then mention that I was trying to get accepted into the program. Each time they responded the same, "Let me write you a letter of recommendation!” And so, two weeks after the Dean told me I was “unqualified” he had five letters of recommendation for me from his distinguished alumni. They described me as someone they were impressed with and who was a good businessman.

I can still remember his call when he asked me to come back in and speak with him. I became the youngest person ever accepted into the University of Houston Executive MBA program. In the end, everyone benefited from my perseverance. I got my MBA in a year and a half and graduated with honors. The University received my money and had another graduate in their alumni promoting the University of Houston. My clients were introduced to the latest in information technology and had a new resource to help them with their future needs. My employer was happy with my sales performance and I qualified that year for my company's top sales award.

My life has been dramatically improved in so many ways because of my experience in that MBA program. The things I learned in class, the people I met in the program, the other graduates I've met since, the doors that have been opened, and the experiences I enjoyed (and endured) have influenced my life forever. It scares me to think what my life would have been like if I hadn't found the courage and the creativity to "Do More."

Wright

Well, what a great conversation Doug. I really appreciate the time you've taken with me today.

Hanson

You bet!

Wright

Today, we have been talking to Doug Hanson. Doug is the CEO of his own company. Doug Hanson Performance Group (DHPG), a company committed to helping individuals and corporations find happiness and success through transformational information and experiences. Doug holds a Bachelors degree in Computer Science from Sam Houston State University and as you already know, holds a Masters degree in Business from the University of Houston. He's most proud of his personal pep squad at home—his wife of more than twenty years, Helen, and his four gifts from God: Kelsie, Cale, Clay, and Kara. Doug, thank you so much for being with us today on *The Game Matters.*

Hanson

I'm "living my dream" today. It has certainly been my pleasure.

About The Author

Doug Hanson is a nationally recognized speaker, consultant, and performance coach who has helped corporations, sports teams, and individuals from all walks of life reach new heights of fulfillment and success. Everyone who meets Doug recognizes his energy and passion for life immediately.

Before starting his speaking career, Doug worked a show director for ESPN sporting events, Director of Operations and Marketing for SuperCross motorcycle racing events, and spent 11 years in the computer industry as an enterprise sales and marketing professional for Toshiba, Texas Instruments and Hewlett Packard, where he was recognized as part of the annual elite sales team seven times.

Doug brings his understanding of human psychology into his presentations in ways that are fun, engaging, and memorable. His consulting group helps companies transform their corporate culture into a thriving atmosphere that nurtures peak performance.

To learn more about Doug and his services, visit his web site at: www.DougHanson.com.

Doug Hanson

3106 Huntington Court

Katy, TX 77493

Phone: 281.391.7532

Fax: 281.391.7539

www.doughanson.com

Chapter Three

GRAYSON MARSHALL, JR.

THE INTERVIEW

David E. Wright (Wright)

Today we're talking with Gayson Marshall, Jr. Grayson serves as president of Balance Your Game, Inc., a ministry born from his heart to equip and change the lives of athletes. He is a former high school and collegiate all-American as well as a record holder. Mr. Marshall now excels as a coach, professional broadcaster, sports consultant, motivational speaker, parenting class facilitator and sports/health consultant. Mr. Marshall is married to a very supportive wife, Darlene, and he has four beautiful and energetic children, Amber, Ciara, Grayson, III, and Devyn.

Grayson, welcome to *The Game Matters*. What is "Balance Your Game"?

Grayson Marshall, Jr. (Marshall)

"Balance Your Game" is a ministry that deals with athletes. I deal from a platform of six principles: spirituality first, abstinence second, life after sports, relationships, stewardship (financially and physically) and dealing with the media. These are the six areas I really believe athletes are struggling in. First of all, what I want to do is to give them the proper understanding of where their gift comes from.

Second: the maintenance of their bodies and their lives. Third: who's speaking into their lives—who's in their inner circle; then, how to deal with success and failure; how to deal with how the world has given them a title to be perceived; and finally, how they truly are perceived as opposed to who they truly are. "Balance your Game" is dealing with the whole man. It deals with the oneness they should have in Christ, the ultimate Gift-giver of their ability—the responsibility they have to give back, whether they feel they have it or not.

Wright

So, how is the game different today than when you were in high school or in college?

Marshall

The way I see it, it's much more commercialized—there's a whole lot more marketing than ever before. That's part of business, but it's a little different from when I was there. Because of that difference, the interest in the game—the interest of younger people to get involved earlier—the magnitude of balance is not being given to young men. They don't have a full understanding of what to do with it—what its full purpose is and why they've been given so much so early. The Bible says, "To whom much is given, much is required," so to whom much is given, much will be asked. Many times there's a fine line between compensation and commitment. Without real wisdom in their lives, they lose sight of why they play the game. We've elevated these guys to a point of iconic idolatry. They take that, absorb it and begin to get a misconception of who they are, so that when they've finished the sport they've dedicated their lives to, they have no idea who they are because they've become what the world dictated.

The Bible says in Romans 12:2, "... be not conformed to this world," or don't be a part of this world, "but be ye transformed by the renewing of your mind." You've got to change who you are mentally. These kids have got to mentally know who they are to be able to deal with everything whenever this is over or whenever they make the transition from star player status back into normal everyday life.

Wright

So why is your message so unique?

Marshall

I think it's unique because nobody wants to hold athletes to task. I think when athletes become iconic entities; folks only want to be around them for what they can get out of them. I've been there, done that. I've had success, I've had failure and my job is to tell them what coaches don't—what they don't want to hear. Nobody wants to do that and I don't have a problem with doing that. I'm not in this to be liked. I've got to tell the truth and I believe if I tell the truth—help folks later on in life—they'll understand what I was doing.

The Bible says in Hebrews 12:6, "Whom the Lord loveth he chasteneth." You've got to have a passion in your heart for these kids and love them enough to tell them the truth, not only on the court or whatever the field in which they're interested, but you have to love them as people. Because when you die, I don't care if you've got a ten-bedroom house on six acres of land, none of that follows you to the grave. So what is your existence about and whose life are you affecting? As athletes, whether we want to or not, we affect lives. The choice now is whether I am going to affect them positively or am I going to affect them negatively.

In the microscopic lens we live under, the way for us to manifest the right light after sports is gone is to have some boundaries, foundations, and some fundamentals. The game is simple, it is still pick and roll, stop the other team from scoring and score more points than them, but because of the athletic ability they have, the game has changed to high-flying dunks, three-point shots and what your team will call "the highlight of the day." They become usable parts and merchandised commodities for which the end result is usually exploitation. You've got to do right by people, you've got to treat others the way you want to be treated and you have to love your neighbor as yourself. Only then can we get out of these guys what I truly believe they should be giving back.

Wright

How has being a Christian affected your plans in life?

Marshall

It totally changed my life. I played the game of basketball not knowing Christ, so I was in it to win at all costs, sometimes. The mantra that echoed permeated my thoughts and directed what I did. As a Christian, now, I understand these six basic principles I deal with, so I have to let them know spiritually where they need to be:

1. Spirituality: Who is God to you?
2. Abstinence: Why you have to keep your body for yourself.
3. Relationships: Who is in your inner circle, who's talking to you, who do you get good counsel from?
4. Life after sports: Are you prepared for when this thing is over? That's an important issue.
5. Stewardship of financial/physical: Are you taking care of your money? Your temple?
6. How to deal with the media.

I think that is what my life as a Christian has done—it's opened my eyes. Now that I'm dealing with conviction in Christ and His focus in my life, I've let a lot of things go. A lot of things I did before Christ don't sit well in my spirit anymore and I think that guys need to know that. They still are going to have a choice to make, but they can't make an informed choice when they're hearing only one side.

Wright

You're almost talking about the before Grayson and after Grayson.

Marshall

That's what my life is. The Bible says in 2 Corinthians 5:17, "Therefore if any man be in Christ, he is a new creature: old things are passed away; behold, all things are become new." I am a different person. I'm the same 6-foot two, 200-pound person to play, but my mind is different, and I truly believe a changed mind makes for a changed man. "For as a man thinketh in his heart, so is he" (Proverbs 23:7).

Wright

So what factors determined your decision to become a Christian?

Marshall

Major failure. Take a look at the book of Job—God allowed the enemy to come in and bring disaster (everything but death) physically, financially and emotionally. I had some major setbacks in my life, but at 28, God resurrected my whole love for the game, my love for people, my love for change. Every record I broke in basketball was for assists and that's all I knew how to do. But because of poor decisions in my life I was in a position to *assist* or help *no one*, even though it was the calling card of my existence. Now that God has lifted me back up—the Bible says when you be lifted up strengthen your brother (see Luke 22:32). Now that God has seen fit to lift *me* up, I can go help other folks.

Wright

So what course and direction do you believe your life would have taken without Christ?

Marshall

I'm afraid to even know. I know where I was headed. I was headed for a good life; I was doing well financially. I'm a college graduate and I think I would have had success, but I would not have had a fulfilling life—all the riches in the world can't give you peace. The Bible says, "Be careful for nothing; but in everything by prayer and supplication with thanksgiving let your requests be made known unto God," (Philippians 4:6) and then He will give you the peace that surpasses understanding.

I live my life for Him, day to day, serving Him and I get peace. And in the midst of all that peace, He takes care of all my needs, just like He promised in Matthew 6:33. "But seek ye first the kingdom of God, and his righteousness; and all these things shall be added unto you."

Wright

So what does it take to be a successful athlete in this day and age?

Marshall

I think it takes Balance. I think it takes coaching, not only on the court, but off the court as well. I think it takes accountability. I know it takes commitment. I know it takes the willingness to give what you need as an athlete. We don't want to do what everybody else does—we're individuals by nature; but when it comes to making decisions, we seem to make decisions in keeping with the status quo. We do all we need to do to become a super athlete—run faster, run longer, work out harder, shoot more shots, study more film and then when it comes to decisions about life, we ask for counsel from other folks who do not have our best interests at heart concerning what we should do.

Wright

I've got a lot of experience parenting—I've got a 43-year-old daughter, a 41-year-old son and a 16-year-old daughter and I've often kidded my friends saying, "I believe God sucks their brains out at 15 and returns them at 20-something."

How do you feel you can directly affect the lives of teens today?

Marshall

I think charismatically, implementing what they need to hear. Like you just said about their brains disappearing at 15. If you train up a child in the way he should go, when he is old, he will not depart from it (see Proverbs 22:6). I think we, as parents need to understand we give birth to our kids and God has a neat plan for each one of their lives. I think what we can do is, if we're more balanced, if we understand more—if we're not drill sergeants but we're empathetic and we have grace—if we're living something before them—I think we can affect positive growth in them. The biggest challenge I have in dealing with young people today is they think their parents are hypocrites. The parents say, "don't cuss", but *they* cuss, the parents don't allow them to drink but *they* drink, the parents say, "don't smoke", yet *they* smoke.

If you want to raise your kids right, you've got to go to their level and what adults have to see is that change isn't just in the adolescent years—change is ongoing. If we don't understand that there needs to be an element of change *daily* in growth and maturity, we will have a hard time when we get older. We need to understand it's really not about us. No—your life is not your own, it was bought with a price and you have a responsibility to those who follow you.

Wright

So what is the attitude of people in sports today? Is it healthy?

Marshall

Money. The general attitude reflects the enormous investment of owners and media. It's become an event— a social gathering—a pursuit of entertainment and I think for the players that the job is something they feel they have to do for the spectator. Again, not all, but the purpose has changed from the love of the game to "the game can provide for me." Not that there is anything wrong with that because they are there to make a living, but the integrity of the game would be maintained if the money and marketing was not the underlying focus.

Wright

Since you've been in involved in ministry through basketball, what doors have opened for you and what challenges have you faced?

Marshall

I have had the privilege to speak to thousands of players and coaches on every level and share the need for balance. However, I do realize that I am a veteran from an element that doesn't fully embrace God. I'm not talking about the players wearing WWJD bracelets or praying after the game. I'm not talking about the fact that some players really don't care. I mean folks standing up and saying, "I love Jesus- stop tripping- leave me alone- it's alright what I do- what y'all do is wrong according to the Word of God. I'm not trying to kill your buzz or be a killjoy but what you are doing right now isn't going to get you any closer to heaven." That's where it is—ministry; and we have to go back- go back into Egypt. We've got to go into some of those dark places and share God where God isn't accepted and where God isn't wanted.

When you introduce God and the gospel people have got to change. The presence of God changes the atmosphere. If you have God in your life, people become uncomfortable in your presence. And they begin to hold you to a different standard and respect the convictions you live by, whether they agree with them or not.

Wright

My wife and I chaperoned about 60 high school kids last week in a five-day trip to New York City and I was amazed at their decorum. I was amazed at how responsible they were and how well they treated each other and people they came in contact with but yet I know that this is a small number of people who represent the school. I know a lot of other kids who are really having a hard time and just getting into all kinds of trouble and all that. What can I as a parent do to not only help my own kid—I take mine to church every Sunday—but what can I do to help other kids who don't hear the right things at home and even the right things at school?

Marshall

Simple. Tell them what's right and keep telling them. Teaching your kids is not just a Sunday event. You could not survive or remain nourished if you only ate once a week. So we can't expect the purposed truth to emanate from their character if they are only exposed once a week. They don't watch TV or listen to music once a week. We are trying to play a game with the deck stacked against us. We have to realize that whatever has their focus has their momentum. Today's youth need to direct their energy to truth. They are truly hungry for it and we need to provide it and not be hypocritical when delivering the message. We have to buy the truth and sell it not. We have to make a concerted effort to meet them where they are in their understanding of the gospel message and at the same time not sugar coat the real truth. Then we follow the verbal by living something before them that sets a standard that is totally opposite of the world today.

And you have to be a haven for them. You've got to share with them—I think that's part of the Gospel message— to tell everyone who doesn't know what they've got to see in your life. Here's the thing about the anointing: when God is in your life folks are attracted.

Wright

How do you work against the media images? For example, I love the game of basketball, I don't think there's anyone appreciates Michael Jordan and the several basketball players—there a lot of great ones—but two of the most famous ones, you know Michael admittedly had a gambling problem and probably the other great player has HIV now. How do you tell kids that only one out of a zillion ever make it to the top and when they do, they all have "feet of clay"?

Marshall

Right now, 550,000 kids are playing high school basketball and less than 50 will make the pros. That is less than one percent. These are athletes with all the ability to make it, but because of *no Balance,* they listen to their fans and have a misconception of who they are. They subsequently live defeated lives even in the midst of seeming success. They have no concept of what God says we should do—"present our bodies a living sacrifice, holy, acceptable unto God, which is your reasonable service" (Romans 12:1). That's why our lives are not our own.

An athlete doesn't understand this, but by the time he's six or seven and his abilities are superior to some other folks' and he progresses to the next level, he never gets a chance to understand what balance is. Nobody wants to give him balance—everybody wants him to be "somebody". What they don't understand is that in Christ you are somebody. When these kids realize that, and they reach their athletic peak in their lives, then they have balance and they stay humble. Humility is what God loves. The Bible says, "Pride goeth before destruction, and an haughty spirit before a fall" (Proverbs 16:18). The word "pride" is used so much in the athletic venue, and those are the words that shape the character of the people.

Wright

One final question, Marshall As you look back over the last few years, do you see that you've made a difference?

Marshall

You know, it's without question. There are so many kids I really believe who have had their lives change. They keep coming back to me and they say, "Coach, thank you so much." But as I said in the beginning, we're working on a 190,000 square foot facility that is going to be the state-of-the-art playing basketball-training field in the Southeast. We're going to have about 20 peripheral services: we'll be feeding the homeless, ACT and SAT prep class, GED completion, jobs skills training, creative writing, job placement, etiquette classes, a sports café, a motivational bookstore, a sports arcade play station, four or five courts in it—indoor/outdoor—shooting stations, racquet ball- it's going to be amazing!

We're going to use basketball to draw kids and we're going to use basketball to draw adults. You can't clean the fish until after you catch it—so the basketball is the draw to catch them. When we catch them we'll clean them, then we can send them back out.

So that's where God has blessed us and been gracious to us and we just look forward to being able to continue to be effective with a lot of people.

Wright

Today we've been talking to Grayson Marshall, Jr., president of Balance your Game. He is a former high school and collegiate all-American and he now preaches, consults; he's a professional broadcaster and motivational speaker. He holds parenting classes and he's a teen consultant.

I think he's proved here today, at least in this book, there's something to this balance. Grayson, I think you've got it together with your "Balance Your Game" and I really appreciate the time you spent with me this morning.

About The Author

Grayson Marshall, Jr. serves as President and Director of Balance Your Game, Inc., a basketball ministry supported by the Potter's House Christian Fellowship of Jacksonville, Florida. Coupled with his commitment to support the spiritual development of youth, he inspires excellence through our youth's natural inclination toward physical activity as a basis for instruction in the teachings of Christ. A former McDonald's high school All-American, Mr. Marshall has excelled as a coach, college athlete and professional broadcaster since his days at Clemson University (starter 1984-1988, Team Captain senior year, All-American in 1987 and 1988 and is the ACC's all time assist leader, a rank he holds at Clemson to this day). Mr. Marshall provides consulting services for Athletes, Motivational Speaking, Parenting Classes facilitation and Teen Court consulting. Mr. Marshall is married to a very supportive wife, Darlene, and has four beautiful and energetic children: Amber, Ciara, Grayson III, and Devyn.

Grayson Marshall, Jr

Balance Your Game Inc.

5732 Normandy Blvd. Suite 14

Jacksonville, FL. 32205

Phone: 904.635.6588

Email: coach@balanceyourgame.com

Chapter Four

PHILIP FULMER

THE INTERVIEW

David E. Wright (Wright)

Today we're talking with Phillip Fulmer, whose first decade as head coach of the Tennessee Volunteers could be classified as the best ten-year period in the school's glorious gridiron history. He led the football team to a national championship in 1998 and was named National Coach of the Year that same year. In 2000, Coach Fulmer received the second annual State Farm Eddie Robinson Coach of Distinction Award. This award is given to a coach for being a role model and mentor to students and to players, for being an active member of the community, and for being an accomplished coach.

The University of Tennessee (UT) has posted ninety-five victories under Coach Fulmer against just twenty losses since he was named head coach in 1992. His winning percentage of 82.6 percent also places him ninth all-time in Division 1A, alongside such notables as Newt Rockney, Frank Leahy, Barry Switzer and Tom Osborne. In fact, he's the only coach in the top fifteen on the all-time list who is still active. His efforts have been especially fruitful of late. Tennessee has led the SEC during the last five years with a total of fifty-two victories.

Coach Fulmer is the author of two books: *Legacy of Winning*, written with Gerald Sentel, and *A Perfect Season*, written with Jeff Haygood. Coach Fulmer brings a relaxed but motivational style to corporations who want to inform and inspire their employees and keep customers with game plan success. He does a lot of speaking throughout the United States. Coach Fulmer, welcome to *The Game Matters.*

Phillip Fulmer (Fulmer)

Thank you very much.

Wright

Coach, many corporations today find one of their biggest challenges is creating an environment of success in the workplace. When you speak to the business sector, how do you advise companies to do that?

Fulmer

I think one of the most important factors is taking the role of a leader, setting the standards high, and guiding all the employees down a path of distinction. In other words, everyone in the organization knows the goals that are set and the attitudes that required to get there.

In our case, we tried to establish an "all for one and one for all" type of attitude and work with our long-term goals in mind on a daily basis. I think it's extremely important to have that as an atmosphere within the "family," if you will.

Wright

Do you have great communication with all your assistant coaches? What are your methods of communicating with them?

Fulmer

I think we have great communication. That's a very important part of what we all do to be successful. You've got to believe that the team is the most important factor. In our situation, we're dealing with youngsters who have different maturity levels and often with varying strengths and weaknesses and environmental issues. Formulating that into the team concept takes great communication. My leadership role is to give them the foundations and the paths to follow along the way. My assistant coaches and all of the support groups should simply be an extension of me and us as a whole. It's best when you have that consistency and that communication level going; most of the time, you are successful.

Wright

The Sporting News, one of sport's most prestigious magazines, has written of you, "He's a player's coach and a solid motivator. Fulmer is the nation's best coach." What do you think it means to be a "player's coach"?

Fulmer

You know, I had some concern about that initially, because I thought that perhaps that definition made me sound like I was soft. But after maturing some myself in the position, I think it means there is mutual respect and that it runs both ways. I think the players know the consistency I expect from them, the effort that I expect, and the off-the-field expectations as far as academics and social behavior go.

We touch on the spiritual attitude of the young man, because I still think he's in a developmental time. In return, players know they can expect the same determination, the same efforts, and the same examples set by me and my staff. When you're working with that kind of relationship, I think it could be called "being a player's coach." We're not dictators—we're mentors—we're men who are trying to help adolescents grow into men. We take that approach, and it's been successful for us.

Wright

Coach Fulmer, your record indicates some little known facts—at least little known to me. For example, you had a total of sixty-four academic All-SEC honorees in four years, including nineteen in 1998. With all of this talk about college football being about business only, do you believe there's a correlation between an excellent student and a good athlete?

Fulmer

I don't think there's any question that if your team has good players, they are also better students—dedicated and hard working. That doesn't necessarily mean they're all going to be rocket scientists or anything like that but they're determined to have success.

If you have more players like this than your opponent, you are more than likely going to win. I do think there's a correlation between success and academic achievement. You're here to be a student athlete. The truth of it is that our team is, in some ways, a springboard to the National Football League for some athletes who are very skilled. You certainly can't say they're not successful when they make five-million-dollar-a-year salaries. For the most part, there is only a very limited number of guys who are going to be able to do that. The rest are out there to prepare themselves to be employers, employees, citizens, husbands, and fathers. We take that role very seriously and expect the players we have to take it very seriously also.

Wright

To follow up on that question, are academically excellent student athletes easier to coach than students who are not? Will these traits not follow them in the business life after football?

Fulmer

There's no question about it. We're all very interdependent on each other. The guy who's the self-starter—the one who's going to get up and have breakfast, get to that 7:50 A.M. class, makes sure he gets to that study hall in the evening, uses the tutor and does all of those things—is going to be the guy who will be out there hustling and being the "early bird getting the worm." I don't think there is any question that the background taught by their parents and reinforced by us is going to pay great dividends in the future.

Wright

You've stated that the development of good citizenship attitudes is compatible and consistent with team goals. What opportunities do you give your players for community service and involvement?

Fulmer

We have gone as far as to hire full-time staff member Jim Harrison who's responsible for public relations and community service for our football team. He does a tremendous job helping our young people. I think it's so important in their short-term growth that players feel like a part of the community and that the community feels good about them.

In the long term, the communication skills and the appreciation for what they have in college are important because they will often come in contact with people less fortunate than they are. We require each player on our football team to do at least one activity per semester in the community. Obviously, a lot of our players are more high-profile players and do a tremendous amount more than that; but overall, we're very active in giving back to the people. We have tremendous support at UT and we feel like we're a part of the community and that we have that obligation.

Speaking somewhat selfishly, I think that when they're out there reading to a fourth grade class, visiting a sick child in the hospital, going to an old folks home, speaking to a D.A.R.E. group or whatever they do, it makes them more accountable and more responsible for their actions. It has paid great dividends for us also.

Wright

I can remember growing up in the Knoxville city school system. Back when I was in the fifth or sixth grade. I can remember people like Doug Atkins and Jimmy Hahn—I think it was the 1951 national championship team—coming over to our grammar school and teaching us to square dance. I will never forget that.

Fulmer

I don't know if any of our guys will be teaching square dancing, but I'm sure they could teach the dances that are out there now.

Wright

You just don't think of Doug Atkins, that giant of a man, helping a fourth or fifth grader learn how to dance.

Fulmer

It does make a significant impression. I remember the same thing when I was a youngster. Ronnie Warwick, who was a great linebacker for the Minnesota Vikings, came to our school and spoke; he actually spent some time with us. At that particular time, he was the only guy I had ever asked for an autograph; I still have it. It made an impact on me. He told his story and I figured out that if he could do what he had done, considering all the struggles he had gone through, it was something that I could do too.

I hope our kids are motivating young people to go out there and try to be successful.

Wright

As an offensive guard at the University of Tennessee from 1969 through 1971, your team's record was thirty wins and only five losses. Since there are so many players in the sport but so few coaches, it must take a different set of skills to coach. What do you think it takes to be an excellent coach?

Fulmer

I think you have to be multifaceted in today's world—a leader of men but also a communicator, not only with your athletes but also with your staff, the administration, and faculty. Then you have responsibilities with the boosters and the fundraisers and all those kinds of things, so you have to be a great communicator.

I think it helps to be positive. I'm one of those guys who says the glass is half full most of the time—we're going to find a way to get it done. I think that's extremely important. You have to be able to manage your time and set your priorities in order to allow yourself to be successful and make the best use of your time.

I learned the hard way that you still must remember your family. During my first couple of years I was so determined to make it work that I think I drifted apart from my children and my wife. I made a really determined effort to get back and catch up on those years that I missed to spend quality time with my family.

I think that as a tactician and a strategy guy, you've got to be able to plan for the future—figure out the problems before they get too big and change with the times. We've been able to do that with our studies and research. Recruiting is obviously a very valuable tool, and that goes back to the communication skills and hard work. Once you get a good player to the campus, it's really a matter of developing his skills because everybody recruits good players; then the kids who are the most disciplined and the most physically developed mature. Usually the teams with the most juniors and seniors are going to be the most successful teams. This requires that you develop your skills and spend quality time developing that relationship so they're going to respond to what you ask of them.

Wright

On more than one occasion, I noticed your daughter by your side on national television as you ran to the middle of the field after a game. How hard has it been to raise three daughters and a son, given all of the time demands you've had since becoming head coach?

Fulmer

I'm very blessed to have my children. My son is thirty-two, and I missed a lot of time with him; but my girls have been with me at my side. It was my wife's idea to put them at the sideline with us. I was concerned about what they might hear or that they might get hurt; but it's been one of the greatest things for them to share in those exciting moments—and there have been a lot of them—and to share even in the few disappointments we've had.

For them to be there and be a part of what's going on has given them an appreciation for what Daddy does. I think, again, it goes back to the core values of our program and that's one of the ways we demonstrate that family is important—that we're all there for each other and we'll be there whether it's the best of times or the toughest of times.

Wright

As you mentioned, recruiting is extremely important. Besides obvious athletic ability, what characteristics do you and your staff look for when recruiting?

Fulmer

You begin with character, which I think is extremely important. We tell our guys we want character in our program, not characters. Guys are going to go to class when they're supposed to be and they're also going to be in the weight room when they're supposed to be. We're not going to have to worry about what they're doing in the evenings. Of course, college is a growing time and there are a lot of problems out there if guys want to find them, so they have to make good decisions that way.

We talk about them being "line-touchers"—those who are going to touch the line when the coach is not looking. We talk about those things as a staff before we offer scholarships. It's really easy to see the guy in the film who's going to be the next great player athletically because of his size or skill. We call them "twenty-footers" because you only have to watch about twenty feet of tape before you realize this guy is really special. But you've got to find out a lot more than that. Academics, character, the environment, what their goals are, where they come from, what I can expect as far as stability, ability in the young man, and how he will take discipline when it comes down to it—we discuss all of those things thoroughly.

Wright

When I interviewed Vince Lombardi Jr., he said that his father's greatest strength as a coach and a man was his faith in God. The elder Lombardi was, of course, a legendary coach and that surprised me a little. Through the years, has faith played an important role in your decision-making?

Fulmer

I don't think there's any question that faith in God has been probably the key issue in my success. I was raised by a wonderful mom and dad in the church. Men in the community who gave me exposure to the Fellowship of Christian Athletes (FCA) also tremendously supported me. FCA gave me the opportunity to go to Black Mountain, North Carolina, Lake Geneva, Wisconsin, and Snow Mountain, Colorado, to FCA camps. My faith grew there and I was joined with other people of different denominations from around the country who were also athletes. It allowed us to bond and have a support group with each other.

My wife is tremendously faithful as a Christian lady. My children have grown up, thank God, to be the same way with the same values. It's not that we haven't made mistakes along the way. We're certainly not perfect by any stretch of the imagination; but the faith we have together is the bond in our family. I believe it is also the bond in our program. We look for that in young men—not a particular denomination or anything like that.

Wright

I suppose the true test of the influence a coach has on the athletes who play for him is whether or not they stay in touch with him through the years and still call him by that revered name "Coach." Do you keep in touch with your former players, and do they still seek your advice and council?

Fulmer

We stay in touch quite well, I believe. Obviously, you have some who are more special than others just because of the relationship you build and all of the things you go through while they're here in college. Particularly as an assistant coach, I still have a great bond with a whole bunch of guys I got to know as a position coach. Then as a head football coach, I have really learned to make sure I take time to touch base along the way with all our captains and all the leaders on our football team. Peyton will pick up the phone and give me a call, or it might be Peerless Price. Last night at an alumni event, I saw Bubba Miller, one of my great linemen from a few years ago. You might not have seen them for five years or even have talked to them for a year but when you see them it's like it was just yesterday.

Wright

Coach, I have a last question for you. If you could give America's leaders advice on how to be successful leaders, what would you say to them?

Fulmer

We talked about core values earlier. Establish what the core values of your organization are going to be and don't veer far from those.

Communication is also tremendously important because many times we all want the same end but we might take different paths in getting there—sometimes, it might be one of those paths that takes you a lot farther than it should.

I think discipline is extremely important. We often hear, "Coach, you do a great job of recruiting." And we do. But I also think we do a great job of coaching and developing those skills in those young men and having discipline in our program so that we are never too far away from our core values.

Wright

Coach, I sincerely appreciate the time you have spent with me today. It's been fascinating, and I've really learned a lot.

Fulmer

Thank you for *your* time. I appreciate it. Send me your card, I'd like to keep it in my Rolodex.

Wright

I certainly will. Today, we have been talking with Phillip Fulmer, whose first decade as head coach of the Tennessee Volunteers has been absolutely fantastic. Many think he's the greatest working coach in football today and many others I know believe he's one of the finest men they've ever seen. I think we've learned that today.

Coach, thank you so much.

About The Author

Phillip Fulmer is completing his ninth season as head coach of the Tennessee Vols and has continued to add to the list of accomplishments that have placed him in the top ranks of his profession. First and most important to fans of the Vols has been his status as the nation's No. 1 coach in terms of winning percentage. Tennessee's 8-3 regular-season mark in 2000 maintained Fulmer's won-lost ratio margin as No. 1 compared with his peers. But, it was off the field last fall that Fulmer received one of the most prestigious and personally satisfying honors that can come to a man in the field of athletics. A blue-ribbon panel of judges named Fulmer the second annual winner of the State Farm Eddie Robinson Coach of Distinction Award. Named after famed Grambling coach Eddie Robinson, the award honors an active college football coach who demonstrates the qualities that exemplify Coach Robinson's legacy–a role model and mentor to students and players, an active member of the community and an accomplished coach.

Phillip Fulmer

www.PhillipFulmer.com

Chapter Five

Brian Biro

THE INTERVIEW

David E. Wright (Wright)

Today we are talking to Brian Biro. Brian is one of the nation's foremost speakers and teachers of leadership possibility thinking, thriving on change, and team building. Brian is the author of the acclaimed best seller *Beyond Success*, recently number seventy-one on amazon.com, *The Joyful Spirit*, and *Through the Eyes of the Coach: The New Vision for Parenting, Leading, Loving, and Living*. Brian was rated number one from over forty speakers at four consecutive *Inc Magazine* international conferences. With degrees from Stanford University and UCLA, Brian has appeared on *Good Morning America, CNN's Business Unusual*, and *The Fox News*.

Brian, welcome to *The Game Matters*.

Brian Biro (Biro)

David, it's my pleasure to be with you. Thank you so much for having me here.

Wright

You've written four books and travel around the world speaking and teaching about team building, teamwork, life balance, thriving on change, and possibility thinking. What in your background prepared you to do this important work?

Biro

Well, you know that's what really attracted me to the work that you're doing. My background was as an athletic coach when I graduated from college, I was a U.S. swimming coach and that is probably the best ground you could travel to prepare for focusing on bringing out the best in people.

Athletics is such a microcosm of life. You learn how to win. You learn how to lose. You learn how to try and how to work together. I spent eight years focusing every ounce of my heart and soul on building these kids, and our team became one of the largest privately owned swim teams in the country at that time.

Our team achieved many things, but what I learned most of all was that there's something special in each person. That's really what coaching is about. You don't really coach a sport first—you coach *people* first. That background prepared me for what I do today.

The only reason I ever left coaching was because I had no life—I had no balance—all I had was my work. So I made a decision to go to the Graduate School of Management at UCLA and work for my MBA, and ended up going on into business. I rapidly came to understand that the things I learned in the athletic arena were just as pivotal in business. To this day I still feel that I'm a coach. I just don't get quite as wet.

Wright

One of the strangest things I have observed in my life that I've known and still know about getting things done is that balance is still not understood. Many of my collegiate and pro coach friends know about getting things done—they know about coaching and everything, especially life coaching—but they still don't understand balance, do they?

Biro

It's huge! My life's biggest lesson has been learning how to create and maintain balance. Even when I sign my e-mails I always keep balance and priorities foremost in my mind. My signoff says: Brian Biro, Husband, Father, Speaker, Author.

For me, it's crucial to keep that balance and perspective. Many people believe you must give up success to find balance. I actually believe it's the pivotal and often missing key to having great success not only in your career, but also in your life.

Wright

One of your mentors has been the great coach, John Wooden of UCLA basketball fame. Tell us about Coach Wooden and some of the most important principles you've learned from him.

Biro

I think it's very appropriate we're talking about Coach Wooden today because tomorrow will be his ninety-fourth birthday. Coach Wooden is a shining light, not only for those in athletics, but also for everyone. I think perhaps the most important thing I've learned from him is how important it is to "walk your talk." There's a simple but revealing statement that says, "You can judge the quality of a person by the way he treats those who can do nothing for him." John Wooden passes that test with flying colors. He is a gentleman. He treated his players, coaches, alumni, and the press with dignity and respect. He was unusual in a several key ways. As I talk about these differences it's important to remember that Coach Wooden was the most successful coach by far in the history of his sport. No other coach in the history of men's basketball has won as many as four national championships—Coach Wooden won ten!

Wright

Right.

Biro

But here is where you start to see the Coach Wooden difference. Though Coach Wooden is very pleased with his accomplishments, he'll be the first to tell you that he coached for twenty-eight years before he won his first national championship. He says things like, "It's what you learn after you know everything that makes the difference." He was always hungry to learn something new and knew there was something to learn from each person. So that's one key difference.

A second was the definition of success he by which he lived. In twenty-seven years at UCLA, the greatest coach in college basketball history never said the words 'winning' or 'losing' to his players. Not once! Now that does not mean he didn't want to win. He did. But what he taught instead was that "success is peace of mind and it comes from knowing that you've given the best of which you are capable." By living according to that definition he focused on what you put into the pursuit, to the process of doing your best. He wanted his athletes to focus on what they controlled, which was themselves—their attitude, their preparation, their energy, their team attitude—rather than focusing on that which they didn't control. That's a huge difference, and one of the major secrets that separated him from all others.

Another key Wooden difference is a perspective from which we all could learn. Almost all coaches I know tend to coach backwards. What I mean by that is when we seek to correct an athlete, we show them what they are doing wrong and focus most of our attention on clearly analyzing and describing what they are doing poorly. Coach Wooden used a process which I call the "sandwich effect." When athletes were doing something incorrectly, Coach Wooden first showed them what was right. The subconscious mind records what you show them, so he wanted them first to see the right method, the right thinking process, the right technique to use. Then he showed them what they were actually doing.

That is important because as any athletic coach would tell you, many times our perception of what we're doing is not accurate. Here's an example: As a swimming coach, I would often seek to correct athletes who had fallen into the habit of using a stiff, straight arm recovery rather than a relaxed bent arm technique. Virtually every time, the athletes were sure their arms were bent. Their perception does not match reality. So it's important that they truly understand what they are doing.

And then lastly, Wooden showed them what was right again. So it was like a sandwich. He was two to one in the ratio of really embedding in their mind the correct procedure or the correct action. And there are a million more things about him, but he is, to this day, a shining light of wisdom and class. He lives his principles every day. He's just an incredible guy.

Wright

In your best selling book, *Beyond Success*, you suggest that our thoughts, beliefs, and expectations create a magnetic-like attraction. Can you give us some tips on how to use this understanding to help our children, friends, and co-workers to improve confidence?

Biro

Absolutely! The concept is called the "Pygmalion effect." It says that our thoughts, beliefs, and expectations create a magnetic-like attraction in the direction of those thoughts, beliefs, and expectations. A researcher has actually proved this. He went to first grade classrooms and told teachers he had developed a test for the children that would identify for the teachers which of those students were what he called "spurters." A "spurter" was a child with lots of ability but who had not used that potential yet. So he administered this test, and when it was done, went back to the schools and told the teachers which of the kids had scored as spurters. But it was a fake. He never graded anything. All he did was completely at random select kids and tell the teachers they were the spurters. Well, guess what? Those kids who were selected at random spurted because the teachers looked at them differently. The teachers were looking for their potential. The teachers were looking for that part of them that was exceptional.

So how do we use that as parents? Well, it goes back to that sandwich effect we just talked about. The first thing we do is put more things in the positive when you're raising your kids. It is amazing to me how many of us focus most of our conversation, most of our teaching, and most of our parenting pointing out what they are doing wrong. This is with the very people we love the most! The first step in understanding the power of the Pygmalion effect is to focus on what's right, on their strengths and improvements. It doesn't mean that when they make a mistake or an error in judgment, you ignore it. But your emphasis and direction must be clearly in the positive. How often do you say, "don't forget" instead of, "remember"? What you focus on is what you create!

It is critical to understand that we communicate most of all not through what we say but rather through our body language. I learned this as a coach. A favorite story I tell often in my seminars is about a young athlete who I coached the same way for eight years. I loved her, wanted the best for her and may have even said the right things to her often—but my body language was saying she just wasn't that good.

How transformational the Pygmalion effect became when I woke up enough as her coach to figure out, "Hey, I need to look for something different if I am going to help something different come out of her." When I opened my eyes in this new way I became an entirely different kind of Pygmalion. She soaked in that positive spirit and blew by all those limits I had placed upon her. With our own children we've all wondered at one time or another, "Why don't these doggone kids come with an instruction manual?" That's why it's so important when you're working with kids as a parent, coach, or teacher to start by really examining your own beliefs about them and to look for their strengths rather than spending all of your time trying to correct their weaknesses.

Wright

All the great managers work on their athletes' strengths rather than on their weaknesses.

Biro

It's tremendously important because if you don't, you're always in a position of damage control. By contrast, when you work on others' strengths, they already feel good about what they're doing. And so you're going to enhance that confidence which will ultimately have a bigger effect on helping them with their weaknesses.

Wright

In your books and seminars you help us discover how to elevate our energy. Can you talk about this critical key to a richer life-expanding energy?

Biro

First of all, why is energy so important? It's important because to your children, to your co-workers, to your teammates, to your family, and to anyone in your life you care about influencing in a positive way, your energy *is* your example. People will remember very little of what you say, but they'll remember your energy.

The first key to elevating your energy is simply to become clear that your energy is your choice. So often we forget it's *our choice.* Most of us look at our own energy the same way we look at the weather. It's like, "Hope the weather holds up for my tee time Saturday." Isn't that the way we often look at our own energy? "I hope I have enough energy to make it through this week." "I hope I have enough energy to get through these three meetings today." It's a life-changing key when you realize not only that your energy is a choice, but that you can also cultivate that choice.

There are three keys to elevating your energy. Number one is to change the way you move. Isn't it interesting that people we admire because they are so sharp in their later years are those who keep moving mentally and physically? I love the statement that says, "People don't get older, they just stop moving." So that's number one—physical vitality changes the way you think and feel. Somebody asked me once, "Well, are you saying, Brian, that energy makes you smarter?" And I replied, "You know, I wish I could say that, but I can't. I will say this: energy lets you access more of your smarts."

A great way to work with your energy is to evaluate it on a ten-point scale so you have a context that makes it easy. Then ask yourself this question: On that ten-point scale, with one being comatose, and ten being the way you feel when you are absolutely at your best, where are you living your life on that ten-point scale? Great question! To elevate your energy, pay attention to that scale and change the way you move at key moments when it's important to be more alert, more aware, and more alive!

The second way to elevate your energy is to ask yourself better questions. Questions like, "What am I truly grateful about today?" "What's my most important next step?" "What will I change or improve in myself today so that I can be a better example to those I love?" Questions are a great way to access your energy.

The third and most powerful way to increase your consistent energy is to focus on your *purpose* every single day. Have you ever noticed how much energy you have when you're full of purpose? When you've got a project that's got to be done, something that you are excited about doing, energy is no problem even if you hadn't had enough sleep. When we lose sight of our purpose we lose our energy.

The challenge is that most people don't look at their purpose very often, maybe once a year with a New Year's resolution. Looking at your purpose once a year is like going to the gym once a year. You know all it's going to do is get you really sore. But if you look at it every day, that purpose becomes so much a part of what motivates you—what inspires you about who you are—that your energy starts to rise and elevate. It really makes a dynamic difference.

Wright

You're a big believer in reaching out to others and letting them know just how you feel. How can a simple "thank you" make a difference?

Biro

I like to call that "World-class Buddy-thanking." Probably the most important thing I could do to answer your question is to ask a question. Who are the people in our lives we tend to forget to thank the most? Almost everyone I know answers, "The people we're closest to."

Wright

That's right.

Biro

It's our family and it's our co-workers with whom we work side-by-side every day. We all know what happens—we take them for granted. It becomes a habit. So the concept of becoming a *world-class buddy-thanker* is a fun way to shake us free so we open our eyes and don't let a day go by without letting them know in some way how much we appreciate them, how much fun they are, and how much they mean to us. This is huge. Probably the most important statement I've ever made is, "The love we fail to share is the only pain we live with." If you don't break the "taking people for granted" habit, the love you fail to share will be the only pain you'll leave with.

Here's a simple and fun way to become a world-class buddy-thanker. It's also very appropriate to our focus today on sports. Simply remember ESPN. The "E" means to thank people for their "Effort" and "Energy," not just their results. We've been conditioned to only give acknowledgment, recognition, and praise after the job has been done, the goals been achieved, and the games been won.

Now, don't get me wrong. You still acknowledge for those accomplishments. But even more, acknowledge people for their efforts, energy, and attitude. We've all had times where we've given our best but did not reach the goal that had been set for us. But the funny thing is, if you thank people for their effort and energy, guess what? They'll create more results because now they're focusing on what they do control. So the "E" is to thank people for their effort and energy.

The "S" represents a principle I've never heard anywhere else. This is an exclusive *The Game Matters* secret! The "S" stands for "Surprise." Use the power of surprise to acknowledge others. Surprise stays with people. It can be as simple as an unexpected handwritten card or an elaborate event you take months to plan. The power of surprise however big, however small, is a very powerful transformational way to express recognition and acknowledgment. Surprise shatters patterns and lets people see what they've been missing about themselves.

The "P" is the most important one of all. It means to be fully "Present." When you're with people, be there 100 percent mind, body, and spirit. Our most important job as parents, coaches, teachers, and leaders is to be sure that everyone we serve *knows* they are important. Your presence expresses to others more powerfully than words that they are important. So the "P" in ESPN is a wonderful reminder to be fully present.

Finally, the "N" in ESPN is to practice world-class buddy-thanking *now*. We may never pass this way again. If you had twenty-four hours left, and God had told you that's it—that's all you've got—who would you absolutely positively make sure you told how much you appreciated them, how much they mean to you, and how thankful you are that they are in your life? And the question that brings the importance of "now" home, of course, is: What are you waiting for?

Wright

Whether in business, family, or sports, you speak of the secret behind the secrets. What is that foundational principle?

Biro

It is the "P" in ESPN--the power of being fully present. Sometimes we don't see the power in something until we look at its opposite. When I was a young executive in my corporate life, I was not present for my family. I thought I was doing it for them. I worked all the time and was never around. Then one day I was driving to work at 4:40 in the morning, as I did every day, and all of a sudden I realized that my little five-year-old daughter had stopped running to me when I came through the front door. It used to be that she couldn't wait to tell me how much she loved me, couldn't wait to tell me how excited she was to see me, and couldn't wait to tell me all the things that happened all day—and I've got to remind you that when you're five years old, cool stuff happens.

Wright

Oh, yeah!

Biro

But I missed it because I was not present. My mind was back at the office thinking about the meetings I had been in all day or worrying about where I was flying to that weekend. That morning I got a great gift from God. God woke me up and said, "You know, the past is history; the future a mystery, and the gift is now. That's why we call it the 'present.' " And I realized that the greatest gift I will ever give to anybody I care about is to be fully present for them whenever they seek my presence. Because what it communicates to someone is, "You are important!" When you're not present, you speak equally as loud. What my little girl was thinking from my lack of presence was, "I guess my daddy doesn't care about me as much as the stuff he's always thinking about."

So, how do you become more fully present? Inch by inch, anything's a cinch. Pick out one person in your life who for thirty days you commit to be more fully present with. That doesn't mean you have to spend more time with them. You may have less time in those thirty days. But when you're with them, shut off the television. When you're talking with them on the phone, stop doing your e-mail simultaneously. Ask them a few more questions. Listen more. As you become more present, a fresh new energy will emerge in your relationship. And if you're more present with one person, it will extend to the next person, and the next, until you establish a new habit. We cherish people who are fully present because they're the ones who impact our lives. You just know that they care about you. And it's not so much what they *say* that makes the difference—it's when you want them to be there for you, you know they're there.

Wright

What are some of the other most important principles to instill in organizations, teams, or families to build great support and teamwork?

Biro

Well, I think one that is extremely important is the principle called "blame busting." Blame—b-l-a-m-e—is the single most destructive word in the language of teams and families. I'm not saying people don't mess up. It's what you do when mess-ups happen that makes the difference. The reason blame is such an insidious destroyer of relationships, teams, organizations, and families is simple. When you think of blame very practically, in the context of time, is blame about the past, the present, or the future? Blame is always about the past!

Any time you become mired in blame, you're stuck in the past. Can you do anything in the past? Heck no. That's done. So by cutting blame off at the pass and becoming a blame buster, you break out of the past where you have no opportunity to make change, and move to the present where you do have the opportunity to make things better.

Blame busters stop dwelling on what's wrong and simply say, "Okay, what happened? Get clear about it. This is how we screwed up. This is what didn't work. This was my poor choice." Then they immediately accelerate into the present by asking, "What are we going to do *now* since we have that information and can now do a better job." This is tremendously important in organizations because where blame is rampant people are terrified of taking risks. Why? Because when blame is embedded in the culture, every time you take a risk, it hurts.

Wright

That's right.

Biro

And if you want to have a great team, especially in a world that's getting so much faster, you want people who are willing to take good risks, who are willing to stretch and go beyond where they've gone before. To make that happen, you must adopt the principle of blame busting.

Another important key to really helping organizations is "sub-group busting." I have a lot of fun with this one in my seminars and joke that in many organizations you have operations, sales, and administration. The operations team hates the sales team! But that's all right, because the sales team hates the operations team. The only thing sales and operations have in common is that they both hate the home office a little more!

One simple question will change all that. It's a crucial question to ask often in every team sport, which includes business, family, and community. The question is: "Who is the team?" The truth is, as soon as you take that question to heart, the answer is clear. Sales people realize they can't fully succeed without operations. And the operations people know they need sales people if the organization is truly going to thrive. Finally, both operations and sales understand how vitally important the home office administration is if everyone is to win. Sub-group busters value differences. They are the visionaries who don't want to have everybody on the team think just like them because they understand that when you bring different strengths and perspectives together you create a richer whole.

One last key in building teams and organizations is to recognize everyone as a leader at certain times. There's a concept that goes, "it's amazing what's accomplished when no one cares who get the credit." Organizations that recognize that concept will thrive on change and excel in the toughest times. Credit is something you give. Responsibility is something you take. When we build that understanding into our teams and families, watch out!

Wright

You state that we're all leaders. Most of us have been raised to think that there are few leaders and many followers. In fact, I've read many books that say two percent of this nation are leaders and the other ninety-eight are followers. Can you tell us about your *fresh* perspective here?

Biro

When I say, "We're all leaders," the truth is we're all *self*-leaders. What is leadership? Ultimately at its base, leadership is essentially making decisions. Any time you make a decision, that's an act of leadership. So the first and foremost reason why I really believe we are all leaders to some degree is simply that we're all self-leaders. We're the CEO of our own lives, and I believe we have the capacity to make new choices and make new decisions and to put ourselves in the game. One of my favorite quotes comes from the "Great One," Wayne Gretzky. He said, "I missed 100 percent of the shots I never took." That's brilliant. Notice he's not talking about *making* the shots. He's talking about *taking* the shots.

Wright

Right.

Biro

The choices we make determine what kind of example—or Pygmalion—we are: positive, negative, or neutral. Like it or not, we are all teachers. How do we handle adversity when it arises? How patient are we? At what level of energy are we living our lives? How do we deal with difficult situations, and difficult people? How do we deal with success? When we have young children we see that we are leaders because we realize how much what we do is going to be reflected in the way they see the world. The truth is we are having a similar impact on people around us as well. That's the chief reason that we're all leaders.

There is another reason: We never know when our moment may come. I call it the 'WOO,' the "window of opportunity," when a choice we make, a statement we make, an action we take, an action we don't take may be the one that could affect another person's life so dramatically that a life on its way down completely turned around. We never know if something we say at just the right moment enables a person to see what they couldn't see without someone else's eyes. So the fact is, we're all Pygmalions, and that means we are all definitely leaders.

Wright

In your seminars, you're well known for having participants break through one-inch thick wooden boards as a personal break through experience and an incredible team event. I think our readers would love to hear about this break-through approach.

Biro

It's so much fun. I must tell you, I've led board-breaking experiences more than a thousand times, and I never get tired of it. It's so inspiring! I believe that we are all break-through coaches with the opportunity to help our family, friends, and teammates break through from fear to freedom, from failure to faith, from impatience to patience, from good to great. We want to help our kids break through and make good choices that keep them away from drugs, or decisions that can really affect their lives negatively. I also believe as Confucius says (and as Coach K at Duke loves to paraphrase): "When we hear we forget. When we see, we're more likely to remember. But when we *do* we understand."

In my seminars I want to give people an opportunity to have these real-life, break-through experiences. Everyone writes down on their wooden board something they truly want to break through in their life. For example, the first time I ever broke a board I wrote the word 'procrastination.' And for me it was procrastination about writing books. It was very specific. I always wanted to write books, but I always found a way to put it off. I'd tell myself, "I'll do it when the kids are older. I'll do it when we have more money." The only reason I didn't write my books was one word—fear. "What if I can't?" "What if I write it and it's so terrible nobody wants to read it?" That's what kept me from writing my books.

It is the meaning you give to your break-through metaphor that creates the power in the experience. By writing the word 'procrastination' on the front, it represented everything that was keeping me from living my dream. On the other side of the board participants get to be kids again. They get to write down what's waiting for them when they've broken through that limit—fear, obstacle, habit, or doubt. I wrote, "Freedom, abundance, and truth to my own word," on the opposite side of the board from "procrastination."

Everyone identifies a very personal meaning to his or her break-through. It's also so much fun because the process of teaching board breaking teaches people how to be at their best when their best is called for and teaches them about balance—physically, mentally, emotionally, and spiritually. It teaches them about real teamwork because people are clapping and cheering. The unconditional support is *amazing*.

So picture a room 500 people. There are fifty circles of ten people each and one individual in each circle who will hold the board for each participant. Everyone is clapping and cheering your name! The place is shaking, energy is soaring, and music is pounding. When each person breaks his or her board, it is such a moment of clarity and focus and celebration! For many people, it's the first time they've ever had a room full of people cheer for them ever in their lives. Some people have grown up thinking, "I'm not very physical." And so the act of breaking through is huge. For many people it's what they've written on the board that means the most. But by far the biggest impact that comes from the board breaking is to recognize that often we will cheer more for others than we'll cheer for ourselves. Often we will get more impacted and emotional when somebody else breaks the board which teaches us that unless we fill our lives with the power of teamwork, we miss out on our true break-through potential.

Wright

One of your other intriguing principles is about becoming a "master asker" if you want to be a top-notch leader, teacher, coach, parent, or human being. What's that all about?

Biro

Well, that's a fun one because most of us have been raised with the belief that you go to a leader for answers. Now, there's a time for answers. There's a time for teaching and instruction. But I'm going to suggest that today more than ever before, great leadership is more about questions than answers. Questions are the keys to helping people think for themselves. Questions are the keys to helping people discover their vision and ultimately, questions are the way that you can assist people to take ownership or "PR," *personal responsibility*, as I call it, for their contributions to their team.

Secondly, every one of us has what is termed the "reticular activating system" in our brain, or the RAS for short. The reticular activating system is a net-like group of cells at the base of the brain. It's the part of the brain responsible for filtering out most stimuli from getting through to our conscious awareness. That's critical because there's so much stimuli going on at any moment that if you didn't have something that blocked out most of that information you'd go on overload—you could not concentrate. The RAS lets in what is of value to you and what's a threat, and it blocks out everything else. So what's that got to do with questions? Here's the answer: When you ask great questions, you turn on the reticular activating system. So when you ask your teammates questions like: "What's the greatest team you've ever been a part of? What made it such a great team? How did you feel to be a part of that team? What did you receive from that team? What did you contribute to the team?" and you listen to their answers, you get your RAS in gear (pun intended!). Through the combination of great questions and the RAS you'll be so much more aware of how you can provide things—to your team mates, to your family members, to the people that you're leading and coaching and teaching—that really make them tick. So, questions are a great way to ignite the reticular activating system.

Another reason why questions are so crucial to great leadership is that questions allow people to discover their own motivation. I appreciate but chuckle to myself when people say that I'm a motivational speaker. I'm a *motivated* speaker. I *love* what I do.

The only motivation that lasts must be internal self-motivation. I can't impart that to somebody by telling about it because I don't completely know what's going on inside of him or her. But I can ask. I can ask questions that allow them to identify for themselves what inspires them. I can ask questions to get them to see clearly where they want to grow and improve, and by doing so I assist them in developing internal motivation.

Wright

At the heart of your work there are three break-through tools. What are these and how do you help us achieve break-throughs?

Biro

The first is called vision. We hear a lot about vision, but what are the most important principles about vision? Well, if you want to grow—if you want to improve, if you want to change—the first step is to create a new vision, to see what you want as real now, even though it's not yet come to manifest. The challenge is most of us use our memory to see instead of our vision. In all of my seminars I will ask people a question that always creates a huge amount of surprise. It's a really silly question, but I'll ask them, "What color is a yield sign?" Close to ninety-five to ninety-eight percent of them will say the same thing—"Yellow." Well, yield signs are red and white. They've been red and white forever. And they laugh because they've seen thousands of yield signs.

They've seen them but they really haven't seen them. Why? Because they don't use their vision to see, they use their memory and their conditioning. We've been conditioned because most of the other road signs are yellow and black, so we stop looking. Well, that's fine for yield signs, but what about when we look in the mirror? What about when we're looking at the people in our lives? We may be doing the same thing—using our memory to see whom we are and not recognizing that at any moment we can make a new choice and change. So break-throughs start with vision.

Vision, however, is not enough—it's a powerful start; but when you combine vision with the second break-through tool you ignite momentum. That second tool is called "personal responsibility"—"PR"—which is the greatest birthright we've been given. We've been given about 800,000 hours here on earth. What we do with those hours is called our life—our personal responsibility. What's great about that is to know that we don't necessarily control everything around us. We don't. But we *do* control our reactions and responses to those things. When you add a personal responsibility to vision, you begin to move your life by choice instead of chance.

The third break-through tool is the one that I call "the accelerator." It's also the one that makes life fun. It's the power of "*Team*." With just vision and personal responsibility we can get a lot of things done, but the truth is, when we embrace the concept of "team"—when we recognize and appreciate the differences in people around us, and when we have a purpose that's bigger than ourselves—that's when we really find our ongoing motivation and inspiration.

When we utilize vision, PR, and TEAM in our families, businesses, schools, and sports we create tremendous break-through potential. I really believe that there is something special in each of us. The joy in life is to work to bring it out in everyone you care about, including yourself.

Wright

Today we have been talking to Brian Biro. He's one of the nation's foremost speakers and teachers on the subjects of leadership, possibility thinking, thriving on change, and team building. As we have found out this morning, he must be using those degrees from Stanford University and UCLA because he sounds like he knows what he is talking about to me.

Thank you so much, Brian, for being with us today.

Biro

My pleasure, thank you.

About The Author

Brian Biro is one of the nation's foremost speakers and teachers of **Leadership, Possibility Thinking, Thriving on Change, and Team-Building**. Brian is the author of acclaimed bestseller, *Beyond Success!*, recently #71 on Amazon, *The Joyful Spirit!*, and *Through the Eyes of a Coach—The New Vision for Parenting, Leading, Loving, and Living!* Brian was **rated #1 from over 40 speakers at four** consecutive INC. Magazine International Conferences. With degrees from Stanford University and UCLA, Brian has appeared on *Good Morning America, CNN's Business Unusual*, and the *Fox News.*

Brian Biro

1120 Burnside Drive

Asheville, NC 28803

Phone: 828.654.8852

Fax: 828.654.8853

Email: bbiro@att.net

www.brianbiro.com

Chapter Six

MARK PEARCE

THE INTERVIEW

David E. Wright (Wright)

Today we're talking with Mark Pearce. You may have seen Mark interviewed on one of the major networks or read his story as told by countless sports magazine writers. Although it's not Mark's nature to be self-promoting, his gifts—emerging ever stronger through the system—set him on a path to success.

Told by doctors to prepare to live his life in a wheelchair, he began to fight and went on to claim the title of World Champion Weightlifter twice. Not only is Mark an athlete but he is also a published musician/songwriter and author.

Being an athlete himself led him to found the youth organization, "Club Impact." This organization's goals are to "Build a child into a leader" by encouraging children to excel scholastically as well athletically. Young athletes in the organization are taught the basic fundamentals of their chosen sport. The coaches, who are hand selected by Mark and the Impact Board of Directors, then mentor the young athletes using sports as a platform to install important life skills. They are directed to build character through community services and integrity in their relationship with adults and each other.

Mark hosts an annual awards banquet to acknowledge those who accept this challenge.

From insurmountable obstacles, Mark Pearce has learned and taught others about their "moment of impact"—those decisive moments that determine their life's course and success level. He's a member of the Ten-Time Texas State Champion—1999 and 2002 National Champion and 2001 World Champion, Team Fitness Weightlifting Team. Individually, Mark has taken the 2002 and 2003 Texas State Champion, 2002 and 2003 National Champion, and holds the 2000 and 2003 World Lightweight Weightlifting Championship. Mark holds State records in two weight classes.

He is executive director and co-founder of "Unconventional Speakers," a unique speakers' bureau. Outstanding lectures have been birthed through Mark Pearce's struggles and victories. His burning desire is to share what he has learned about beating the odds to inspire hope to those who may be facing a moment of impact. As a speaker, audiences are charmed by his humor and inspired by his passion to instill in his listeners the mind of a champion.

Mark, welcome to *The Game Matters.*

Pearce

Thank you.

Wright

So how does a champion think?

Pearce

The mind of a champion is very unique. A champion does not accept mediocrity. The first thing a champion thinks is, "second place is not an option." A champion will tell you, if you're comfortable with second place you've never won first. I know this is contrary to the way we teach our children. We teach our children as long as you try your hardest, then that's all that matters. For an average minded person this is right and very good advice. We teach this philosophy because we don't want to be let down when we fail to achieve our ultimate goal—we prepare our minds to accept inevitable failure and sure enough, that's what happens.

I remember hearing a coach explain to his baseball team they needed to learn how to lose. As I listened to him I understood his intention but I still don't know why we need teach our kids to lose.

Justification of failure is easy to find in today's society. Everyone can find a reason for their circumstances whether the result of a bad childhood or traumatic events that have taken place in life. A champion refuses to accept anything less than the ultimate goal. When a champion fails to achieve success, he will re-evaluate techniques, training, and all other aspects of preparation to achieve a different result on the next attempt. This is how we need to teach our children and young people to handle failure. Don't justify it—fix it so you don't fail again. It is our responsibility as parents and mentors to teach children and young people how to think for themselves. We should teach them the basic concept of looking for solutions to fix problems, not accept defeat.

A champion allows no room for thought of failure. A champion's mind is solely focused on one thing—winning. A champion thinks failure is the option; winning is a choice. Anyone can opt out and fail—it takes no effort to fail whatsoever—but it takes a making a choice to say, "I'm going to succeed." That's how a champion thinks daily—he chooses to succeed.

A champion does not allow his self-concept or personal value to be determined by others' opinions. I've learned very few people will actually rejoice with you when you begin to succeed. It's as if they slowly fall off the train on the journey to success. We have support when we begin talking about the journey. As the journey carries us to various stages and levels of planning and preparation, it is as if suddenly those in our cheering section begin to have second thoughts. As we begin to gather opinions and ideas, some of our cheering "passengers" who were so excited at the beginning now have some doubts as to the practicality of our dream.

It's interesting to see that most negative opinions come from those who were never willing to pursue their own dream. You've met these people; they always have an argument as to why you need to stop dreaming and live more practically. They always find reasons why you are going to fail. Fear is one of the leading killers of dreams. For some, it is easier to give in to fear and refuse to pursue that burning desire inside to live an adventure. Over time, these people become like robots just walking around fulfilling a pre-determined duty with no emotion and no passion. I've looked into the eyes of many dreamless people. They have an empty, unsatisfied, hopeless stare. They exist but they are not "living." An adventurer has a burning desire to look down from the top of the mountain instead of look up from ground level. A champion wants to be the first to look down from the top.

A champion trains the mind to be self-motivating. A champion does not make decisions according to others' opinions of him. If I were to listen to all the voices telling me how hard weightlifting is on my joints or how unhealthy it is for me to train the way I do, I would never have won any competitions, much less two World Championships. I was willing to pay the price because I want to look down from the mountain at all the others giving up as they try to climb. Very few people can breathe the air at the top of the mountain. The higher you climb, the thinner the air becomes. If you are trying to carry someone up the mountain with you and they don't seem ready to keep climbing, you need to set them down before they drain you of your strength. Few truly desire to pay the price necessary to conquer the mountain. That's why you have to understand, your value and self worth or ability to succeed is not contingent on everyone's opinion of you or your abilities. Find the champions and listen to them because they have already been where you want to go.

I remember starting a business and having "friends" laughingly ask, "So, Mark, how's the new business going? Making any money yet?" That kind of taunt alone destroys more dreams and hopes of success for many. A champion has settled the question of self-worth and is not swayed by negative input from others.

A champion believes adversity is a challenge that can and will be accepted and defeated. Yesterday's adversities create experience that will fuel our confidence for the tests tomorrow. There is an historical account of a young boy who faced a seasoned warrior who stood more than nine feet tall. History records that this giant of a man was clothed in heavy armor and was feared by all the soldiers as he stood and mocked his enemies and issued a challenge to face him. Out of all of the qualified soldiers, none dared to step out and face the giant. But, one young man with confidence in his past experiences chose to stand up and defy the laughs and scorn of those soldiers who were too afraid to stand up themselves. The interesting thing about this account is that when the young boy stepped onto the battleground, the nine-foot-tall soldier began to laugh and mock his adversary's size. Even then, this young man not only faced the giant, but he exercised a very important quality of a true champion—he *ran* toward his enemy. What courage that must have taken!

Champions know that adversity and trials stand between them and their goal. The sooner you face your adversary, the sooner you reap your reward. When you have a giant standing between you and your dream, run out to meet that giant head on and use your experience and confidence to propel you to success. By the way, after trying on other warriors' armor, the young boy finally said, "I'm not used to this armor. I will use the weapons that I have proven effective against other adversaries." This young sheep herder took a smooth stone and a leather sling shot, and due to years of sharpening his skill against bears, lions, and wolves preying on his sheep, he hit that giant warrior between the eyes and cut off that giant's head with the giant's own sword.

Trust your experiences to aid you when adversity comes. Sometimes, we can't wear someone else's opinions and experience—we have to rely on our own.

Wright

How large a role does pressure play on the competitive stage at the world level of competition?

Pearce

Pressure plays a very persuasive and decisive role. I've competed against many athletes who appeared to be more qualified than I was. They looked stronger, bigger, and more muscular. The winner is usually the one who can control their emotions and repel negative thoughts.

I shared a historical account of a young warrior who was on his way to face the enemy in hand-to-hand combat. It is recorded that this young warrior took a moment to kneel down in a brook to find smooth stones for his sling. His experience had taught him that smooth stones fly straight and true while jagged stones are inaccurate.

I believe, as this young man knelt in the small brook, he no doubt took a moment to see his reflection in the pool of water beneath him. He probably looked into the reflection of his eyes and prepared his mind for battle—that was his "brook moment" that I term the "brook experience." We all experience the "brook" every time we are faced with a crisis—it is the decisive moment when you choose to fight through and find a solution to your situation or else you accept the option of doing nothing and falling into a state of mental dullness and hopelessness.

Pressure can impact us in so many various ways. There are times when pressure seems to squeeze the very breath out of us. Pressure can cause physical sickness. Pressure will always demand a response and there are only two responses available: Choose to face your giant head on by refusing to give up, or kneel in defeat and live with a sense of failure.

I said previously that a champion does not allow himself to think about second place. I have failed to win while competing. I've failed to achieve some of my ultimate goals. The difference in my mindset as a champion and those who *expect* to fail anyway is this: when I fail to succeed, I know I gave my all. I did not cut corners because there was no doubt in my mind that I could succeed—I trained hard—I had all the information and the proper technique. Failure motivates me to train harder and smarter for the next competition, making necessary adjustments in technique or mental preparation. Failure is not final—it is simply a warning that we need to re-evaluate our technique and training.

My experience with pressure was an eye-opener for me. When I won my first world championship in 2000, I learned a great deal about pressure and how it can affect even physical strength. As I began to digest the reality of having to succeed on my third and final attempt in order to win the world championship, I remember that in my mind I began to think of all kinds of reasons why I did not deserve to win and one of my opponents did. I reminded myself of that one repetition I was too tired to complete in the gym—one out of thousands completed as I prepared for the championship. I heard myself saying, "See Mark, you cut a corner. You don't deserve to win this. All these other people here, you know they worked hard, you know they didn't cut corners, you don't deserve this." You have to win the battle with your mind when you're under pressure—pressure not to believe the negative that even your own mind can present to you.

Then there's the pressure of looking at your competition and believing they're more worthy to win than you are because they might have a better look. I'm five feet and ten inches tall and weigh competitively 195 pounds, so most lifters, including some women, look bigger than I do, in my opinion. In that aspect alone your mind will play games with you and that's why there are four things that can help you excel under pressure.

Number one: You have to trust your trainer. My trainer is a seven-time world champion. He's been power lifting for more than thirty years now and has taught me to stick with the plan, focus, and motivate myself. Many times, he is whispering in my ear before a big lift saying, "Mark, you can win, you will win if you want it—it's in the mind." A necessity in living a successful life is having a "trainer" or mentor who truly wants you to succeed and has already been a success themselves. Very few unsuccessful people truly want to see you succeed to a level beyond their own success.

I compete against hundreds of competitors and many of them tell me, "Good luck," as I step onto the platform. Do you honestly believe they want me to succeed? Of course not, because that means they get second place. What competitor at any level wishes their competition to have good luck and beat them out of first after training all year to be champion? Again, that's why a proven, successful trainer is so important to your success. Your trainer *wants* you to win and has prepared you to win. You can trust your trainer.

My trainer has experienced and overcome every level of pressure I'll ever face in competition. With that experience, he is more qualified than I am to understand the necessary preparations to achieve success. Sometimes he makes suggestions I totally disagree with. I've learned to listen, however, because my trainer truly knows more than I do. If he didn't, I would need to find a new one.

The second thing you have to do is trust your training. During the competition I mentioned earlier, I was thinking about that one repetition I didn't finish. You can't do that—you have to focus on all the repetitions you *did* complete. You have to focus on the fact that, "I *am* prepared for this challenge or I would not be here today." So you *have* to trust your training. Remember what I said about pressure producing doubt in my own abilities? A champion will say to himself, "You've trained long and hard for this title and you are well prepared to achieve this goal.

In life, we have situations arise that affect us positively and negatively. I consider each of these moments as training sessions. They may weaken us for a time but as we heal, we will ultimately emerge stronger, wiser, and more confident to face the next moment. I've often thought of some of my previous trials and difficult moments. At the time, they seemed to be life-and-death situations; I stressed over them tremendously. It's amusing how minute they seem to me now that I've overcome them and face new challenges.

I recall my parents and grandparents often smiling at me when I was a young man, as I would zealously impart my opinion on various situations. Often I was telling them a better way to accomplish a goal. I realize today the smiles on their faces represented the humor they saw in my inexperience and ignorance. Time and age change perception and techniques. Proper training can save years of frustration and heartbreak. If you are willing to trust your trainer's experience, you will achieve success much sooner than you would on your own.

Thirdly, you have to trust your technique. Learning the proper technique can mean the difference in lifting 700 pounds. When you're on stage and all the pressure is on, you have to believe and trust your technique. Trusting your training means you believe in your technique. Trusting your trainer assures you that you have learned the proper technique. When you fail to succeed, always take a moment to evaluate your technique. Proper technique is a very vital tool in every aspect of your life. Regardless of your profession, technique will determine your level of success. I tell all of my audiences, "Always evaluate your technique and be open to adjust it when you are not achieving success." Show me someone unwilling to change his or her technique and I'll show you someone who will soon be outdated. In business, being outdated will cost you everything. Never be too proud to make a change; after all, it will benefit you in the end. If you are achieving a high level of success, don't be too quick to try the next new idea either. Balance your journey with an open mind to change yet maintain loyalty to what works.

Wright

So, how do you emotionally deal with pressure?

Pearce

You must believe in yourself and not rely on accolades from others to motivate you. You have to realize you deserve to be on that platform—regardless of were your platform is—you deserve to be there. You have to believe that all the aspects of your life and your experiences have brought you to this place because you're ready to handle it. You have to convince yourself you *can* handle it. Some would say this sounds conceited but when you are under the weight of intense pressure, it is crucial to believe in yourself.

Wright

So how has being a world-class athlete affected your daily life?

Pearce

Being dubbed as a world-class athlete has deepened my commitment to continue to improve. It has impacted every facet of my life even beyond competing. Where I used to focus on going to the gym to work out, I now have narrowed my focus to very specific muscle groups that will make me even stronger as I build them individually. I want to maintain being a world-class athlete. I train every day—when I'm tired, when I'm sick, I still go to the gym. I have a habit of working out—it's my daily routine.

Achieving success as a world champion has presented opportunities to meet many people and speak into their lives. You quickly realize younger people look up to you. They expect you to carry yourself a certain way, with integrity and honesty. You have to understand that because of your accomplishment, people expect more out of you and you have to accept that responsibility.

Wright

How do you motivate yourself when you don't feel like training?

Pearce

I motivate myself by remembering a past experience. At age twenty-five I was diagnosed with severe rheumatoid arthritis and rheumatic fever, and was told to prepare to spend the rest of my life in a wheelchair. For nine months I could not lift myself. After a lot of prayer—and I believe a divine intervention on my life—all the symptoms left my body—they went away—so now, when I don't feel like going forward, I remember those nights when I would crawl through my house. I think about someone telling me I would never walk again. I think about the intense pain I experienced burning every joint in my body even when I took a breath. That is all the motivation I need.

Wright

And how is your health now?

Pearce

My health is perfect—I have a clean bill of health. My doctor looked me in the eye and said these words I'll never forget, "Mark, you have no guarantee these symptoms will not return. They could return in a day, in several months, or even in several years. Live large with the time of good health that you have." My battle cry now is a direct quote from that doctor, "LIVE LARGE." I decided to begin weight training to defy the symptoms of arthritis. I could not even lift myself when I was ill but now I have the strength to lift four of me!

Wright

What attributes does a champion possess that give them the drive to excel beyond the average?

Pearce

I think these are common words people use but number one, they have a strong will. I call it "stubborn faith." Stubborn faith says regardless of what anyone else says around me or what obstacle I must overcome, I know I can do it. I believe everyone has the heart of a champion inside. You can do it, you will do it, and you have to believe that—you have to hear that voice in your mind louder than any negative voice saying you can't. When someone tells me I can't, that's all the fuel I need to drive me forward. I can and I will. That's one attribute.

You have to be determined. I am determined. I am determined to go to the gym. I refuse to lose. I have a strong mindset of determination. I am determined to out-train and out-lift my competition. I recall a historical account of a warrior who was fighting the enemy to protect a pea patch. It is recorded that when all of his comrades retreated, this one warrior stayed his ground and continued to fight. He fought so long and hard that his hand locked to his sword from fatigue. Because one warrior stood his ground and refused to give up, it is said that he single handedly defeated several thousand warriors and his own comrades returned to enjoy the plunder of the victory. Champions possess a level of defiance to adversity to the point they are willing to die overcoming it.

You have to have a strong commitment to your cause. I am committed to the cause of winning my third world championship this year. All the things that come with commitment—whether it's training, maintaining a strict diet, taking nutrients—whatever it is, you have to be committed to the cause. You have to sell out so when the time comes you don't want to work out, that commitment kicks in and says, "No, you're committed to this, you need to go."

I like something Martin Luther King Jr. once said. I summarize his statement when he said, "Show me a group of people willing to be committed to a cause and I'll show you a group of people who will change their circumstances." Commitment to the cause acts as your accountability partner. Commitment forces you to stay focused. Commitment demands action.

Wright

You said a moment ago that "failure is an option and winning is a choice." Can you explain to our readers what you mean?

Pearce

When I refer to failure as the option and success is a choice, I truly believe it takes no effort to fail. I've met many people across the world who seem to challenge that statement because they have so much talent and potential, it is almost as if they have to work to keep from succeeding. I'm amused as I meet people and I'm told of this great local lifter who can lift so much more than I can and how he can easily be a world champion. I'm amused because being qualified is only one of many details. I always respond by saying that if you can't get to the battle, you will never be a great warrior. You may be great on the training ground but until you actually pay the price to get to where the battle is, you'll never know how well you'll respond to real pressure. You can have all the talent in the world but unless you act on it, you're nothing more than a highly qualified could have been.

I believe more and more our society tends to give us valid excuses for why we are the way we are and are therefore justified in our failure. I cannot stand hearing professional counselors and doctors blame criminal activity and personal failure on everyone except the individual in whom they are addressing. They say, "Because you had a hard childhood, that's why you're a criminal—it's not your fault." Well, that's an option. You can opt out by saying, "I have had a rough time through life, therefore I choose to do nothing and I'm excused from doing anything because of my hard time." I meet people who work harder at justifying doing nothing than they would if they actually got up and used their skills to do something.

Everyone has had their share of setbacks, whether they were born into wealth or poverty. I personally love to hear other lifters making excuses as to why they probably won't lift to their highest potential the day before competition. The excuses are humorous—they are already accepting defeat before actually trying to win. I find that true champions are never shocked when they win.

I realize I may seem somewhat hard on the matter of our past hurts and setbacks, that they should not determine the decisions we make today; however, being champion-minded means we don't waste our time whining about all the negative events in our lives. We ultimately have to come to the same point in life that those who achieve success have already concluded. This point must be experienced whether you have been in counseling for years or in jail. I call this point, "The Point of Responsibility." This is the point when you cease blaming Mom and Dad, poverty, poor teachers, terrible school lunch food, or whatever other excuse you have used and you determine in your mind, "I accept those hurts or setbacks in my life but *now I choose* to begin changing my circumstances. This is when you begin making the choice to succeed. Regardless of age, race, or gender, you will have to pass this point several times in your life to continue forward.

When I was sick, my option was riding in a wheelchair. I didn't have to do anything to ride that wheelchair; but my choice was to walk again, and because of the choice I made, I had to force myself to do some things—I had to work for it. We can either accept to use the excuses of our past hurts or setbacks and opt out or we can make the choice to learn from whatever has happened in our life—not accept the excuse which may be even justified—and choose to succeed.

Wright

You've spoken many times about the "moment of impact." Would you tell me what you're talking about?

Pearce

These are moments in our lives that are really stamped in our minds. I'll give you some examples using some of my moments. I remember the day my mother and father divorced. I remember watching my father leave our home. That impacted my life greatly—I've never forgotten it. I remember all the things that came with divorce and what I had to deal with as a child. That was a moment of impact for me.

Another moment of impact was the day my grandfather died. He was my best friend. I had the opportunity as a little boy to live on his farm and spend many hours with him. I have memories of him and me feeding the cows, and working in garden. My grandfather taught me many valuable practical lessons about life by using the routines of farm work. I recall very well the evening he looked into my eyes for the last time as he lay dying of throat cancer. I crawled up on his bed beside him and he just stared into my eyes. I watched as tears filled his eyes. He could not speak to me but I heard everything Grandpa was saying to me as he stared into my eyes.

Grandpa had given me a small Timex watch on one of my birthdays and he quoted the commercial concerning the watch. Grandpa said, "Mark, this watch is a Timex and it can take a licking and will keep on ticking." He then said, "Mark, you be like this Timex. When you take a licking, you keep on ticking." I believe Grandpa knew his time was short due to cancer and he was instilling a very valuable principle to me. The evening he stared into my eyes, I believe he was saying, "I've taught you everything you need to be a success. Now go be that Timex." Grandpa died that evening and I use my relationship with him today to motivate me to succeed. That moment of impact could have devastated me but I chose to use it to fuel me to success.

These are moments where you can either just give up, go into depression and choose not to come out or you can draw back and justify your feelings but you can decide that these moments have made you what you are today—you can say, "They've made me stronger." Those are the moments of impact I'm talking about.

Wright

So do you believe that anyone can take those moments of impact in their lives and use them for fuel to excel?

Pearce

I believe we all have moments of impact. That old saying, "Life happens," is so true. We're either in crisis today, leaving a crisis, or headed for one tomorrow—that's life. And we can choose to make those moments fuel to succeed—to help with our choice to succeed—or they can become walls we refuse to climb.

Wright

How about mentors—are there people in your life who have influenced you to choose success?

Pearce

Several people have influenced me. My grandfather, as I've shared, was the greatest influence on my life. He taught me how to relate with people by taking me to his business every day. When Grandpa would walk in to his motor shop, every worker would literally run over to him to shake his hand. They loved him because he treated them with respect. They were loyal to him because Grandpa made sure they were taken care of. Grandpa told me once to always give a bonus. Grandpa also used situations on the farm to teach me lessons. I've written these lessons in a book using them as chapter names such as, "Don't Let the Cow Step on Your Foot," and, "Shoot

'Em in the Hip and Keep On Walking." These kinds of life lessons I learned from Grandpa's experience are the kinds of lessons a true mentor will teach.

I receive correspondence from all over the world—from people who are facing seemingly devastating circumstances. They want to share them with me because they heard my story or saw me on television. I'm amazed at the calm maturity I see in many children who face terminal illnesses. I strive to be like them because they seem so mature for their age. I've been blessed to meet some of them in my travels. To look in their eyes and see the strength they posses as they face overwhelming pain and fear is incredibly humbling to me. When I don't feel like training hard or I want to have a "pity party," I just pull out a picture or letter and am immediately reminded I have been given a gift.

I also have professional mentors in whom I have great respect; I study their habits and techniques whether in weightlifting or business. My pastor, Howard Conatser, is a great mentor to me because he is genuine and truly has great integrity. I watch him meet people in great crisis when they are ready to give up. With skill, love, and a true compassion for their well-being, he gives them hope.

Wright

So tell me how can I overcome my own setbacks and choose success.

Pearce

You must have that "brook moment" I spoke of earlier. In other words, you must make a decision in your own life that regardless of what comes your way—what has come your way already—you are willing to climb that wall. You refuse to let it stop you—you'll be determined and you'll be committed to the cause, whatever your cause may be. Refuse to lose! Every day, get out of bed and determine in your mind you will better your circumstances somehow before returning to your bed.

When I was sick, I forced myself to take one extra step every day before going to bed, ending my day on *my* terms. It is easy to find a voice to justify your option to fail. Don't let a negative self-concept control your life—do something to change it no matter how minor or small the step may seem. I cried out in pain when I took that one extra last step every evening for nine months. I believe that small six-inch movement of one foot forward, accompanied by tears and pain every evening, propelled me to boldly walk up to the world championship platform and lift hundreds of pounds to win not only once, but up to now, twice. Every time I lift that weight I'm saying to arthritis, "I *won*!"

You *can* defy your circumstances regardless of what they may be. This is how you take back control. When depression forces itself upon you, smile. Do what it takes but smile because that smile defies the very essence of depression. It is your way of taking back control. If I were to be stricken and go back in a wheelchair, I would be like so many other great athletes and kids who daily make the choice from a wheelchair to *not* be hindered by circumstance. This is the mind of a champion and there are many champions we will never hear about out there fighting and winning their own battles with adversity. They are influencing their circle of relationships with their positive and determined attitudes in the middle of their own crisis.

You have to have goals in your life—you have to have dreams. Even the Bible says, "Where there is no vision, the people perish" (Proverbs 29:18). I think it's biblical to say that God gives us vision in our life—a purpose—and He equips us, even through the hard times, to fulfill that purpose. We have to say, "I choose to go forward—I don't want to stop." Times get hard; let's all face it—we get sick, setbacks take place—and there's always that moment, that split second, when we decide, "I'm either going to give in and give up or I'm going to have stubborn faith and refuse to give up." Once we make that decision, insight kicks in and we start looking for ways around the wall or over the wall.

Wright

How important is it to influence others—to be a mentor?

Pearce

We have such powerful influence on young people and children by simply carefully choosing the words we say. I'm reminded of the story of Brooks Robinson being told by his Little League baseball coach he was too big and slow to play baseball and he should go play football. I wonder what that coach thought as he watched this tremendous athlete become a legend in the game of baseball?

I remember when I was a six-year-old boy; my grandfather had lost his key in the grass of his two-acre yard. I looked for more than an hour and finally found that silver Ford key deep in the grass. When I took it to my grandfather, he said, "Mark, you have eyes like an eagle." That simple statement caused me to believe I had sharp eyes and because of that I found many more keys and sewing needles.

My band director wrote a letter to my parents when I was in sixth grade. I was being the class clown. I was a trombone player in band and sat first chair but I wasn't trying hard because it came easy to me. I still have the letter today. He wrote, "Mark could be the best trombone player to ever come through this school if he would just apply himself." I'll never forget that he believed in me. Because of his belief in me, I achieved National honors with my music and have performed on television shows that reach every corner of the world—all because someone believed in me.

A kind, positive word to a child from someone they respect can be the very word they remember for the rest of their lives that will encourage and motivate them to keep living and striving to succeed. I believe it is our responsibility to be encouragers and positive role models for everyone we meet. As we get older and rely on the generation behind us to take care of us, we'll appreciate all of the positive motivation we've instilled in them when they care for us with quality skill and compassion. They won't learn it on a video game or in a song; it can only come from us.

With all the negative going on today, our kids need to know somebody believes in them. Somebody expects them to succeed. And that's what a mentor's job is—it's not only to show them "how" but to also to let them know, "I love you unconditionally, I believe in you, I want you to make it."

Wright

So I'll be able to follow your successes, when do you go for the world championship this year?

Pearce

I have a World Championship competition in Reno, Nevada, on November 15 and several state level and national competitions throughout the year.

David

You have a fascinating life and I wish you the very, very best. I'll keep watching to see if I see if I can catch you on television.

Pearce

Thank you.

Wright

Today we have been talking with Mark Pearce. Told by doctors to prepare to live his life in a wheelchair, he began to fight and went on to claim the title of World Champion Weightlifter twice. His burning desire is to share what he has learned about beating the odds. As a speaker, audiences are charmed by his humor and inspired by his passion to instill in his listeners what we've been talking about today—"The Mind of a Champion."

Mark, thank you so much for making time for us today on *The Game Matters.*

About The Author

World Champion Weight Lifter! Mark took the 2003 World Championship in Las Vegas, Nevada! It would probably be enough just to hear about the dedication it took to achieve this goal but he did it after doctors told him he would never walk again. His stories are humorous, as well as, inspirational. If you want an audience to sit quietly and listen.....don't call this man. He will have everyone yelling with the voices of warriors.

Mark Pearce has been married to Tammy for 20 years. They have two children, Darin and Whitni.

Mark A. Pearce

P.O. Box 1750

Midlothian, TX 76065

Phone: 214.384.7956

Email: MarkPearce1@aol.com

www.markpearce.net

Chapter Seven

Bruce Jenner

THE INTERVIEW

David E. Wright (Wright)

Today we're talking with Bruce Jenner. Bruce captivated the world when he broke the world record by scoring 8,634 points in the decathlon at the 1976 Olympic games in Montreal and earned the title, "World's Greatest Athlete."

In the years following his athletic achievements, Mr. Jenner has become a successful and highly respected motivational speaker, sports commentator, entrepreneur, commercial spokesperson, television personality, actor, producer, and author. Mr. Jenner serves on numerous advisory boards such as the Special Olympics. He also serves on the Council of Champions and The National Dyslexia Research Foundation. He is an avid supporter of Athletes and Entertainers for Kids.

Mr. Jenner and his wife, Kris, serve on the board of The Dream Foundation, an organization that grants wishes to terminally ill adults. He has been a guest on *Oprah*, *The Tonight Show with Jay Leno*, and *Regis and Kathie Lee*. He is a highly regarded and successful author. His newest release is *Finding the Champion Within*. Bruce Jenner, welcome to *The Game Matters!*

Bruce Jenner (Jenner)

It's my pleasure, but you know, that title "World's Greatest Athlete" doesn't help my golf game!

Wright

I hear you're a ten handicap.

Jenner

Actually I'm about a three or four right now. I've worked pretty hard on it but titles when you're standing over that six-foot putt with six inches of break doesn't seem to help—it keeps you pretty humble.

Wright

With all these titles—actor, athlete, spokesman, author—I read that you've been named "Father of the Year" by the U.S. Jaycees and have received "Father of the Year" honors from the Southern California Father's Day Committee. Those are impressive honors.

Jenner

That's just because I have ten children. If you have ten children and you're still standing, boom! you get an immediate "Father of the Year" award. I've been very blessed in that department. I have six girls and four boys, ages twenty-three to four. I do the father thing every day and I'm very lucky.

Wright

Those are great honors for a person whose time has been in such demand for years. Has family always been a number one priority for you?

Jenner

Definitely—especially in my type of business where you're out in the public. You get very plastic, very surfacy; but your real life is with your family. That real life—taking the garbage out, carpools, relationships, good days, bad days, and so on. By far that's what I live for—my family and the everyday stuff I do. Then I get out there and motivate people and try to build some businesses.

Wright

While preparing for this interview I got the impression that a commitment to youth has always been important to you, especially the physically and mentally challenged. Is this a response to your own battle with dyslexia?

Jenner

Yes, because I can really identify with these kids. As a dyslexic myself, I tell kids that if you're dyslexic and that's the only problem you have in life, you've got it made—you can deal with this thing. A bigger problem than being dyslexic is a lack of self-confidence in themselves, especially at a young age. When you're growing up and everybody's accelerating in school and doing well, and reading seems to be simple for everybody else, but for you perceptually picking those words up off the piece of paper is tough, you lose confidence in yourself.

In my case that's basically what I did. I lost interest in school, I flunked second grade, and I didn't want to go to school. My biggest fear in life was to go to school because I was afraid the teacher was going to make me read in front of the class. Not only did I have a hard time getting the words off the piece of paper, but also I got emotionally upset because I didn't want to look bad in front of my friends. It just didn't work.

Being dyslexic, however, molded me into the type of person I am today. I always tell kids that if I had not been dyslexic I would not have won the games because being dyslexic made me special, it made me different than everyone else. When I found what I call my "little arena to play in," and that happened to be sports, it became very important to me. I excelled at that. Not that I always thought about being dyslexic but that little dyslexic kid was always sitting in the back of my head outworking the next guy.

I look at athletics in two ways: the athletic body and the athletic mind. I was given okay athletic skills physically, but being a kid who grew up with a lack of self-confidence I found out my greatest gift was my athletic brain. I could outperform people under pressure because my brain worked so well—I could come up with good performance when everyone else was dying. I was better at dealing with pressure and fear and all those types of things than anybody else. So it was an interesting metamorphosis through life.

Wright

Did anyone in your early years ever call you dumb or stupid?

Jenner

No, but I always felt dumb and stupid because I was always in the slower classes in grade schools growing up. Nobody had to say anything—it was more my own internal struggles that I was dealing with.

Wright

I talked with a good friend of yours, Billy Blanks, the other day and I also talked with Les Brown who is a tremendous motivational speaker in the country. Both of these men told me the same story—they were dyslexic and it almost devastated their childhood. They didn't find out about it until they were in their late thirties.

Jenner

I remember in Junior High school one day they gave it a name and said, "You're dyslexic." I wondered if that was bad—if I was going to die from this. It sounded like a pretty bad word. They said, "No, go back to class. Have a good day." That was about the extent of it back then. Actually for a while there it became *too* big a word. If any kid wrote anything backwards they were dyslexic. It became a catch phrase for a lot of different problems. It's calmed down a little bit now. They've been able to analyze things like this. It's not the end of the world if you're dyslexic.

Remember the movie *City Slickers* with Curly and Billy Crystal sitting by the fire? Billy Crystal asks Curly, the old wise cowboy, "What's the secret to life?" He says, "One thing," and the conversation continues on. Finally, later on in the conversation Billy Crystal asks, "What's that 'one thing'?" Curly looks over and says, "That's for you to find out."

That's so true. In life I was lucky at a young age to find this thing called sports. I found that I had an aptitude for it. Sports brought me out of my shell and helped me feel good about myself, which helped my self-confidence problems. The challenge for young kids today who are suffering with something like this is to find their niche in life. That's a parent's responsibility. It doesn't have to be in sports—it could be in a million different fields. Tom Cruise is dyslexic and so is Cher. The list goes on and on and on of people who found their niche. I try to encourage kids to go out there and try art, try music, try acting, who knows? You can find your talent. If it's taken away in one area, it's given to you in another. Your job is to find the other area and then go with it.

Wright

You have a new motivational book out titled *Finding the Champion Within* published by Simon and Schuster. Tell us a little about it and who will benefit from reading it.

Jenner

I think everybody will. The reason I call it *Finding the Champion Within* is when I was growing up I never knew that down deep in my soul I had something special down there. But every time I'd dig down deeper and deeper through athletics, which was testing me in competition all the time, I realized that there was something there, though I didn't even know what it was.

Probably the one thing that gave me confidence in people was going through that long process—going through the games, being able to win, and stand on top of the platform and all that. We all have that champion living down deep inside that gives us the ability to overcome tremendous obstacles in our life and to do tremendous things with our life. But there's a process to finding that. With the book and through my speaking I talk about that process and try to motivate people to basically believe in themselves. That's why I did the book. The speaking is kind of tough because I run all over the United States to primarily speak to sales groups. I also speak to all kinds of groups and talk about finding their champion within. The travel's tough and I'm away from home and all that; but I really enjoy the presentation. It took my performance in 1976 and that great journey I was on. It didn't die back then, it still lives on to help me motivate people and to move people forward in their lives. It may be one line, one sentence, or one word in what I say or what I've written that might spark one person to say, "Hey, I *do* believe in myself and I *can* do these things."

Wright

I remember reading a program that was produced by a company in Waco, Texas called *Success Motivation Institute* with a fellow named Paul Meyer. He did a program called *The Making of a Champion* and you were featured in one of the stories. It was very motivational. *Wheaties* has just commemorated its seventh-fifth anniversary and you're back on the front of the box along with other superstar athletes like Tiger Woods and Michael Jordan. How does that feel after earning the title "World's Greatest Athlete" twenty-six years ago?

Jenner

To be honest with you it's very flattering. Mostly because when I got out of the games I went into the television world, the commercial world, and all the types of things I've been doing over the past years. It's very nice and very flattering to get in the top fifty athletes of the past decade. It's nice to have that in my memory bank. I don't live on it or dwell on it in my own personal life, but it certainly is a nice position to be in. Obviously, I was very proud of that day—it was a great day. I had trained during twelve years of my life for that moment and I came through. I'm proud of that. It's a nice, very positive message—sometimes in our world today we need positive messages.

Wright

You're a highly respected motivational speaker today. What is the message that corporations want and need to hear in today's economy?

Jenner

You have to have a belief system. Two years ago we were riding high. Everything was just wonderful; everyone was making money; the stock market's going through the roof, on and on. Today you need to look at things probably more realistically than you did back then. We had our heads in the sky. Today you have to be a lot more realistic—you can't just wander through life. You've got to take it a lot more seriously, I think, today especially with 9/11 and all the things that we're going through in our country. We get this great shot—maybe seventy-five years on average that we're on this planet and we've got to go for it.

I believe everybody is at their best when they wake up in the morning and they're excited about that day. Whether you're building a business, improving your relationship with your family, or whatever it may be. When you get up in the morning you've got to be excited about tackling that day, one day at a time. You constantly build on these days, day after day after day, and eventually you've really accomplished something—you've moved forward in your life. You've overcome a lot of things. Today we've got to be smart in what we're doing.

Wright

Did 9/11 have any impact specifically on your life or the life of your family?

Jenner

I think probably everybody knows somebody who was in those buildings and lost their life. We have one friend whose husband was in the building. She was eight months pregnant and Daddy never came home. A month later she had the baby; she's a very close friend of ours. I think everybody was affected. You'd have to be a cold, heartless person to be sitting there on the 11th of September and not be affected. I was stuck in a hotel room in Milwaukee sitting there all day long watching everything that was going on. I was just devastated by it. The world changed that day. Our attitudes changed that day. It was a terrible, terrible tragedy but I will say one thing, it certainly has brought our country together. It certainly has shown the world we are not going to tolerate those types of things. You attack us and you got big problems. We've shown a very strong hand and I think our country is dealing with it very well. There's nothing wrong with a little bit of patriotism out there. We have the greatest country in the world and I'm proud to be part of it.

Wright

When you were standing up there with the gold medal hanging around your neck and you hear the band playing our national anthem and you see the United States flag is going up, does that really have an impact on the rest of your life?

Jenner

It did have an impact on the rest of my life in the sense that forever I'll always be an Olympic champion—it's a pretty elite fraternity out there—that's the main thing that it does. When I went into the games I was the favorite; I was the world record holder. It was the last meet of my life, and it was the last time I was ever going to do participate there. But when I walked away, I had accomplished everything in a sport I wanted to accomplish. I broke the world record three times, I had the Olympic record, I had the gold medal, and I was number one in the world for three years. I walked away smiling because I was so happy I could walk away accomplishing everything that I had wanted to accomplish. Very few athletes can do that—walk away saying they did everything in the sport they could possibly do.

It was a great career and now I'm moving on. In my sport there is no longevity to it. I don't go to my friends and say, "Are we going to go throw the shot or pole vault today?" No, we're going to go play golf. After he won the Masters Tiger Woods didn't throw his golf clubs away and never touched a golf club for the rest of his life. I had to do that. I had to walk away from my best friend—my sport. But I realized that, and I knew that when I started. Was it hard? Yes, it was hard. I was the best in the world at what I did. It's like a piano player, for twelve years of his life he sits in front of that piano banging out the music. You get your chance, you go in front of the rest of the world, you play the most beautiful music the world's ever heard and when the song's over with you put your hands in your pockets and you never touch the piano again. That was kind of sad from my stance. It was a bittersweet kind of moment. It was great and satisfying to win, but I was also sad I was leaving my best friend. It was an interesting thing to go through though. I realized the reason I was walking away.

Roger Bannister had a quote about sports and life. He said, "Only in something like running can finality be achieved, but it is not the type of finality that leaves you with nothing to live for because sport is not the main aim in life. Yet to achieve perfection in one area, however small, makes it possible to face uncertainties in the more difficult problems in life." That's a great quote. That's what sports is all about—go in there, compete hard, and then move on in life to the more important things.

Wright

I'm old enough to remember Roger Bannister.

Jenner

He was the first man to break four minutes in the mile.

Wright

Some of the greatest athletes in the world have taken up golf. Michael Jordan is an example. He would rather play golf than basketball. Why is that?

Jenner

It's just a very challenging game. I play on what's called a Celebrity Players Tour. I played one event this weekend up in Las Vegas. There were about eighty guys participating. They call it the Celebrity Players Tour but it's probably ninety-five percent retired athletes. It's just a great game. Even when you get a little older you still enjoy the competition, the competitive spirit, and the camaraderie with all the other guys who are out there. It's a difficult and frustrating game. It looks so simple but it's so difficult to do. It's a great challenge and it's sets a totally different pace than what you're used to. In my days of competing I was in the Olympic arena. I was out there grunting and groaning in training. Golf's just the opposite. You're out there with your friends, you're enjoying the game, and it's a beautiful day. You're on a golf course, a highly competitive, difficult sport and it yet it's fun. You can do it the rest of your life. It's not like you have to give it up in a few years because your knees go. In most cases you can do it until you're seventy or even older.

Wright

My brother was a golf instructor and he took me out. I was a weekend duffer and couldn't play at all. I just went for the fun. He got me out one day with nothing but a nine iron and knocked twenty-five strokes off my game. He told me to throw the rest of them away and just keep that one.

Jenner

He was smart; he knew what he was doing.

Wright

We are trying to encourage people in our audience to be better, live better, and be more fulfilled by listening to the examples of our guests. Is there anything or anyone in your life who has made a difference for you and helped you become a better person?

Jenner

I have to pick the number one person in my life and that's my wife Kris. We've been very blessed with a lot of children. We've been married a long time now. She's my soul mate—the person I spend every day with. Kris is who I talk about everything with. So number one would be my wife. We're very fortunate and have been blessed in a lot of ways. By far, I have to choose my wife. She's been the best—my bud!

Wright

She works with you now, doesn't she?

Jenner

Yes, she runs the offices. She keeps me organized, *too* organized I think!

Wright

I was reading about an old track coach of yours, L. D. Weldon, who is credited with having been the first person to really recognize the great potential you obviously showed later on. Was he a mentor of sorts?

Jenner

To be honest, I'd almost have to consider L.D. like my second dad. I lived in his home in college. He asked me to come out to this little dinky school in Iowa in the late '60's. When you're eighteen to twenty-two there are a lot of things going on in your life. He was a great human being to be around. He was a great person with good moral standing. He gave me good guidance and he was just a great person to be around. He was a character.

He always liked multi-eventers. He actually had recruited me to play football. I lasted about three weeks and had to have knee surgery, so that was a short career. Fortunately, it was the best injury I ever had because it got me out of that sport. He was not a technical coach who just sat there and worked on technique—he was a motivator. He'd help you out with as much technique as I think was possible for him. He was such a great guy and such a great motivator that you didn't want to lose races because you didn't want to let L.D. down. He's had great decathlon guys in the past. He was sixty-five when we met and he'd had a guy in the 1936 Olympic games. His name was Jack Parker and he took the bronze medal in Berlin.

My favorite picture is a picture of L.D. standing there with his fist clenched and he's got his hat on. He always used to brag about every athlete he ever had. We had to listen to every story about every athlete; but he signed this picture, "To Bruce, the greatest athlete I ever coached. L. D. Weldon." To me, knowing L.D. was like a really, really big deal. That was very special. He was a great human being and great for me during those years from eighteen to twenty-two for guidance and that type of thing.

Wright

I remember as a kid seeing Burt Lancaster play Jim Thorpe, the all-American. I jumped every hedge on the way home from the theater—it motivated me.

Jenner

Oh yeah, I remember that. They did Jim Thorpe. They did Bob Mathias, a story on his life. When I started running the decathlon—1970 was my first one—I didn't even think about the Olympics. The reason I got so excited about it is the guys in the past who had won the Olympic decathlon were not just Olympic champions, they almost became part of American history. Jim Thorpe, Bob Mathias, Rafer Johnson, these guys were bigger than life because it was such a tough event. That was one of the motivating factors. As I got closer and closer to the games I didn't care what happened, I just wanted to stand on the same stage as Rafer Johnson, Toomey, Mathias, or all those guys in the past who had won it. It's a tough deal to win.

Wright

After seeing the movie, I read the life story of Bob Matthias. I just couldn't believe it. Have you ever met him?

Jenner

He's a great friend and a great human being.

Wright

What do you think makes up a great mentor? In other words, are there characteristics that mentors seem to have in common?

Jenner

Yes. First of all they have to be giving people. A mentor has to be, I think, of great moral character. I think that's extremely important. It's like what is called the mastermind principle. You find out what you do and what you want to become in life and you go and associate with those people who are doing it. That's extremely strong—having somebody in your life who has been through experiences and who is willing to help you—that's extremely important. You are influenced a lot by your surroundings. It's important to find those good and helpful people and associate yourself with them, from your family, your parents, the kids you hang out with, the other adults you hang out with. It's extremely important. Who are the people you're looking up to? It's important in life.

Wright

You've influenced so many people around you. I've talked to your daughter a few times. Does she work in your company?

Jenner

Yes, four years of paying for college and she works for us! She started for us four years ago but she's looking at other options now so I don't know how long she'll hang out with us.

Wright

Most people are fascinated with the new TV shows about being a survivor. What has been the greatest comeback you have made from adversity in your career or life?

Jenner

Overcoming the dyslexic problem would probably be it. The old saying, "Success is not measured by heights attained, but by obstacles overcome." There are also some little things like, for me the biggest fear was going to school because I was afraid the teacher was going to make me read in front of the class. I hated that. I sat there with sweaty palms all day long in fear that it was going to happen.

Cut to years later. I go to the games, I win the game and I get a job. What's one of the first things I had to do? TelePrompTer work. I panicked. That little dyslexic kid is my mind. But I was able to go out there and I found my own way to get around it, to be able to do those kinds of things.

I used to host *Good Morning America* when David Hartman or one of the others was gone. That was two hours of TelePrompTer reading, on and on. For me I overcame more to do that than I did to win the games. It was little things like that along the way.

I have to say I really lost interest in a lot of things in the middle '80s. Then I met my wife. We got married eleven years ago and being with somebody you love gives you more reason to work. It's no longer just about working for yourself. I didn't care that much about it—I hadn't worked for years. But finding somebody and renewing the family, adding more kids on to the family, starts to kick you in the butt. I had to start getting serious about life again. It's not just about little old me because I don't need that much. But now I've got a family and a four-year-old and a six-year-old. It motivates you to get back out there and get some things going.

Wright

When you consider the choices you have made down through the years, has faith played an important role in your life?

Jenner

Yes, to a point. I believe in God and go to church, not regularly, but I go. I believe God gave me a life, gave me some talents, some not so many talents—the give and take kind of stuff—to do what I can do with. And then the rest is up to me. My success or failure is going to be determined by myself. I take personal responsibility for my life and I've always felt that was important. I always felt like I had God-given talents with good points and bad points. My job is to use those things, to get out there and make something of myself—to wake up in the morning and feel good about myself is my responsibility. I can't say, "Oh I failed and it was God's will." No, I failed and it was *my* problem. Or, "I was successful and it was to the glory of God." I always feel like I worked hard. God gave me some talent and I'm the one who worked hard and if He's looking down on me and saying, "You did a good job," that's all I need.

Wright

In reading about you, I was interested in the Longevity Network. Are you still involved in that?

Jenner

Yes, we're a network marketing company based in Henderson, Nevada. We sell all kinds of products. We've been doing this for eight or nine years.

Wright

Is it all health related?

Jenner

We do health related things and we do hair care products—all kinds of things for home-based business entrepreneurs. We have a vitamin program, weight loss programs, all sorts of stuff.

Wright

I interviewed Dr. Mendel the other day and he was talking about the health revolution. It was like a war to him. He said each year about 140,000 Americans die from adverse effects from prescription drugs and almost one million are injured due to dispensing errors. He said people are going to have to take control of their own life and their own health in terms of vitamins, running, exercising, and those sorts of things.

Jenner

I certainly agree with that. We have to take responsibility and again it comes down to it's your responsibility to take care of your health and eat properly. Honestly, it's not that difficult. It just has to be a priority.

Sometimes we don't take our health seriously until something goes wrong. Then it's the wake up call. To me, eating properly demonstrates the eighty/twenty percent theory: Eighty percent of the time you eat what normally you would think of as good food. The other twenty percent of the time you have fun—have a little Haagen Daaz, a little of this and that; you can have a little fun with those things. But eighty percent of the time you have to eat right.

Exercise is interesting. The CDC came out with a study back in '96 I think it was basically saying that living a sedentary lifestyle is as hazardous to your health as if you smoke. That's pretty scary, but that's the bad news. The good news was that a moderate amount of exercise, just a little bit of exercise, has as positive effect on your health just as if you're a marathoner. So the good news here is that a little bit goes a long way. That's an important study.

A lot of the reason that people don't exercise is that if they're living a relatively sedentary lifestyle, they think doing exercises is like running 10k's because that's what they see people doing. They say, "I could never do that." But *can* they walk up three flights of stairs instead of taking the elevator. You certainly can do that. Just do a little and realize you don't have to run marathons or go to the gym five times a week—you just have to live an active lifestyle. Get as much exercise in your daily life as you can. If you're in an apartment or your office is on the fifth floor, don't take the elevator up—walk up. Everybody always looks for the closest parking place for the grocery store. Find one that's far away and walk. There are a lot of ways just to get some activity in your life, which is going to have a very positive effect on your health.

Wright

Speaking of health, I remember reading about something you had created called *Personal Blood Storage, Inc.* What is that all about?

Jenner

Back in the late '80's or early '90's a friend came to me and said he was starting this business called *Personal Blood Storage.* Basically what he had developed was the technology to store blood at seventy degrees centigrade below zero. They had been able to freeze blood because it's an individual cell freezing process instead of an organ. If you try to freeze an entire organ it's cell on cell which breaks itself up and doesn't work very well—at least not yet, they'll probably figure it out someday. But they've been freezing blood for years. The problem was they didn't have freezer capacity; they only had small freezers. So he developed this technology in which he was going to do personal blood storage. It was a very interesting entrepreneurial effort.

The concept was so much better that the blood banks that are out there now. In each freezer we could store about 45,000 units of blood. The blood system in the United States doesn't use a freeze technique. The Red Cross is a monopoly and it doesn't freeze blood so every thirty days it has to turn over the blood supply. That's why they're constantly asking for more. I can tell you, the first two weeks of January the Red Cross will be on the news saying that we need blood because for the last month because of the holidays nobody's been giving blood so the system is out and there's no reserve of blood.

So *Personal Blood Storage* offered the ability for you to put your own blood away if you wanted to. Over a year period you could put four or five pints of blood away, store it, and if you ever needed it, it's there so you have your own blood. Or start to build up a reservoir and a supply of blood on the side so in the case of a tragedy you would always have blood available.

Well, as I said, the Red Cross is a monopoly. The poor guy trying to set up this blood freezing program spent a lot of money and got shut down everywhere he went. It was ruthless. The Red Cross came after us because they didn't want the competition. So after about five years of spending a lot of money and trying to fight the Red Cross in every trench he finally said he'd had enough.

Wright

The reason I was so interested in it is that just last week someone was telling me that if I ever had any kind of surgery and had some time before I had the surgery, to always go in and donate my own blood so that there would be no chance my body would reject it. Is that the basic principle?

Jenner

Yes, it's your own blood. Why would you want to transfuse someone else's blood if you could use your own blood? The concept for it was fabulous except you're going up against a monopoly.

Wright

It's encouraging that you still go mountain biking, run on the track at Pepperdine, play golf, are a commercially rated pilot, and race cars professionally in the Grand Prix events. That's pretty cool.

Jenner

I live a very active life and I enjoy doing a variety of things. That's why I was a decathlon guy.

Wright

If you could have a platform and tell our audience something you feel that would help or encourage them, what would you say?

Jenner

The keys to success in life are found in basically four words: gamble, cheat, lie, and steal!

- *Gamble*—Gamble your best shot in life. Dare to take risks. Life has got to be a great adventure or it's nothing.
- *Cheat*—Cheat those who would have you be less than you are. Surround yourself with positive people, uplifting people—people who want to see you do well. Turn around and help them and you're truly a champion.
- *Lie*—Lie in the arms of those you love. When it comes right down to it that's all we have is one another. Never take the love you give or the love that you receive for granted.
- Steal—Steal everyone with happiness. Live every day as if it's your last because we never know when that day is going to come. Gamble, cheat, lie and steal.

Wright

That's great advice from a great American. We have been talking today to Bruce Jenner who literally captivated us all when he broke the world record in 1976 in the Olympic games and he's still at it as we have just found out. He's not only an athlete, but he is also a great businessperson and a much requested speaker.

Mr. Jenner, we really appreciate your being with us today on *The Game Matters.* It's been a personal privilege for me.

Jenner

It was a lot of fun. It was great having a chance to talk to you.

About The Author

After winning a gold medal in the 1976 Olympic Games, Bruce Jenner has gone on to winning seasons in life. He's known to millions as a motivational speaker, TV personality, sports commentator, commercial spokesperson, entrepreneur, actor, producer, and representative of companies such as Visa, MCI, Coca-Cola, and Anheuser-Busch. Jenner travels around the country speaking to corporate and community groups about finding the champion within, and he runs several successful businesses with his wife, Kris. The Jenners live with their five children in Hidden Hills, California.

Chapter Eight

TODD SWINNEY

THE INTERVIEW

David E. Wright (Wright)

Today we are talking with Todd Swinney. Todd has been involved in the sport of bodybuilding since 1978, and became an active competitor in 1980. As a teenage competitor Todd envisioned a fitness center with a full functioning nutritional center as part of the total operation. The nutrition center and fitness center would function as one, and therefore would be able to cater to all the needs of the individual clients regardless of their goals or levels of fitness. The results produced for the individual from this type operation would greatly exceed the results produced by commercialized, mass marketed, one-size-fits-all programs. In January 1993 Todd opened just this type of operation. Maximum Fitness functioned fully as this type of an operation. In 1996 Todd took his operation, knowledge, and clients one step further when he joined forces with the top ranked International Federation of Bodybuilders (IFBB) Professional Bodybuilder Kevin Levrone and his World Gym Fitness Center. Currently Todd works his magic in Millersville, Maryland, which is just one mile from the former World Gym location. Todd welcome to *The Game Matters*.

Todd Swinney (Swinney)

Thank you—it's an honor to be here.

Wright

You have developed an outstanding reputation and a strong following as far as a nutritional consultant and professional fitness trainer is concerned. Could you give us a little of your background and tell us how you started in the business?

Swinney

Certainly, and I will be happy to. First and foremost I owe so much to my parents for their love and support in what I chose to do. My dad is the finest man I know, and my mom was the speaker, writer, communicator, and motivator extraordinaire. She would be thrilled with this project, but God called her home March 28, 2004, so I'm dedicating this to her and her memory. I would not be who I am nor where I am without the talents she gave me. My beautiful wife, Kristen, is my rock, my support, and my best friend. She keeps me focused and on track and I couldn't live without her. That being said, this all started back in March of 1978, when the guy I consider my lifetime best friend, Richard Grissom, brought a copy of the magazine *Muscle Builder Power* to school. Today we know that magazine as *Muscle and Fitness* and it is widely circulated. We anxiously thumbed through those pages looking at the physiques of the outstanding bodybuilders of that era including Arnold Schwarzenegger, Frank Zane, Robbie Robinson, Franco Columbo, Boyer Coe, and all the superstars of that day. We assumed that when these guys went walking through a mall somewhere they got attention.

Now, we were juniors in high school at the time, and that was of fundamental importance to us—that we be the center of attention and turn the teen girls' heads when we went somewhere. I went to the store where my buddy had purchased this magazine along with Arnold Schwarzenegger's first book called *The Education of a Bodybuilder*. At that time they shared with Richard and me that there was going to be a grand opening of a new fitness center there in Florence, Alabama, not far from our hometown, Phil Campbell, Alabama, and that a pro bodybuilder named Casey Viator would be there attending that grand opening.

We attended the grand opening and met Casey Viator. I was seventeen years old and was five feet seven inches tall and he was five feet, seven inches tall. I weighed 120 pounds—I was that proverbial skinny kid, the guy in the Charles Atlas ad who would get the sand kicked in his face. Casey Viator, being the same height as I was, weighed 220 pounds. He had a girlfriend on his arm (and this is the honest truth) who was a "playmate of the month" or "pet of the month," I won't go any further with that; but she was attractive needless to say and that sure got our attention!

At that point, we knew that bodybuilding was for us, and that is where it all began. We stopped participating in our high school team sports, even though we both enjoyed them; but ironically, as soon as we did not participate in the typical team sports, our small town North Alabama High School did not consider us "athletes" anymore, and we were forbidden to use the weight room! We had different opinions however, and would find our way into the weight room sometime during the school day. We would unlock one of the windows and then literally hide away until most everyone was gone. We would then go in through the unlocked window and pursue our workouts! As soon as we could afford it, we joined a gym.

The gym we joined was called Ron's Gym, owned by Ron Russell there in Sheffield, Alabama. We started working out feverishly—the best we knew how—in order to modify our bodies and change our physiques for the better. Ron took an immediate liking to us and took us under his wing. He had been Mr. Alabama in 1959, '60 and '61 and Junior Mr. America in '61 and '62. He is still one of my best friends to this day.

It was during this early phase, during my first year of working out, that I saw such tremendous progress and tremendous results with the limited knowledge I had. I started digging deeper and I started progressing a little more quickly than most of other folks in the gym. People started coming to me for advice. I was very honored and flattered to have that happening because I was one of the younger people in the gym and just starting down this path of body modification.

It was at that point I really visualized the concept for Maximum Fitness, as you mentioned, which was the health club I opened in 1993. I put this concept on paper when I was eighteen years old and shared it with Ron, the gym owner. I told him that this was what I was going to do one day.

It eventually happened. Of course it took several years. It was not always a lifetime pursuit of mine, but it did happen in 1993 with the assistance of a great friend of mine, John Parrillo. John and I had become acquainted back in 1987. I was a competitive bodybuilder still looking for the magic and John supposedly had the magic. I called him one day and we just clicked from that very first phone conversation. Still today he is one of my closest personal friends and I have to give him tremendous credit for being a mentor to me over the years. He's the best and I'm grateful to have been able to follow in his footsteps. I would not be who I am or where I am without his never ending guidance.

I competed as a bodybuilder from 1980 until 1990. Remember, I was 120 pounds when I first walked into that gym; when I stepped off the competitive stage and finally hung up my posing trunks I weighed 215 pounds, so I had really put 100 pounds of muscle on my body during that period of time.

I can't tell you exactly what happened but something clicked in my mind one day and I just really didn't want to compete anymore. I thought it would just really be nice if I could assist other people and help them along their path, whether it was as a competitor, for general health, body modification, or whatever it might be. So, I started Maximum Fitness there in 1993, I began freelance writing and to date I have been published in *Muscle & Fitness, Flex, Ironman, MuscleMag International, Oxygen, Muscle & Fitness Hers, John Parrillo's Performance Press,* and *Exercise for Men Only*. I am very flattered that these magazines—the very ones who put me on the path to doing what I do and being what I am, now—contact me to do articles and interviews. That still somewhat blows me away. I consider myself that same little guy from North Alabama who just likes to help people. I do, however, get to live vicariously through my oldest son, Justin, who is now twenty-one and becoming a very good bodybuilder, trainer, and nutritionist.

My oldest daughter, Kristen, at sixteen, is now preparing for her first NPC fitness competition and she has been cheerleading since age six. I guess you could say it somewhat runs in the family! My other daughter, Stephanie, age fourteen, has been cheering for ten years and has won every award imaginable in that area of competition. Jacob Todd, who is fourteen, is an honor roll student and has played baseball, basketball, and is currently more into motorcross than anything else. Our little guy, Michael, age eight, is a real bruiser on the football field and I'm already anticipating the day he will sign that NFL contract!

I was very honored to be in the bibliography of Dr. Cliff Sheats' *Lean Bodies* which is the best book ever written on nutrition for the average person. Through the course of the last several years I have been very honored, privileged, and blessed to have worked with many world class and professional athletes, not only from the body building, fitness and figure community, but my work has come to include major league baseball and NFL players as well as Olympic athletes, endurance athletes, and the exciting lineup of pro "rasslers," known as "wrestlers" to the rest of us! Once again I have to say I feel very fortunate to be able to do something I love and something I am passionate about as a career.

Wright

You mentioned that you have worked with several top professional athletes. Can you drop some names?

Swinney

There are a few names I can drop and some I can't due to contractual obligations. You mentioned Kevin Levrone earlier. Kevin was my first client to ever turn pro back in 1992. He retired from competition in 2004, and has relocated to California now to pursue an acting career. We still talk just about every week now. The first three athletes I worked with who turned pro were all local Maryland people who worked out at my gym. I turned out three pros in two years from Maximum Fitness, which was really coincidental. One was Kevin Levrone, the other was Theresa Hessler who was one of the very early fitness pros back in 1995. The other was a fellow named Ivory "Papoose" Turner who won the Lightweight Nationals back in 1995 down in New Orleans and turned pro.

Looking at bodybuilding fitness and figure many of the top names I have been privileged to work with including: Carol Semple when she had her Olympia win the Fitness International Champion at the Arnold Schwarzenegger show in 1997; Angel Friend when she turned pro; Stacey Hilton, Fitness Girl who turned pro; and Lisa Marie Varon who is now Victoria in the World Wrestling Entertainment (WWE)—I was dealing with her she got her pro card.

I have assisted many other people in bodybuilding, fitness and figures like Adela Garcia-Friedmansky, Lydia Haskell, Tina Forlifer, Mary Ellen Doss, Vinnie Galanti, Susan Meyers, Mellisa Coates, Renita Harris, Deidra Pagnanelli, Kelly Ryan, Stacy Simons, Jennifer Goodwin, and Lee Apperson. Lee is a popular name in bodybuilding when he won the Mr. Universe title. One of the big names in the NFL was Kevin Greene who retired a few years back; I was actually working with him as early as 1990. He started his career in Los Angeles with the Rams and retired from the Panthers a few years ago. Mike Bilecki from the Atlanta Braves was a great, great closing pitcher for the Braves in the mid and late nineties when they were having all their World Series wins. Tony Saunders, pitcher for the Florida Marlins when they won the World Series, is one of my clients is a local guy from here in Maryland. Chuck Evans, fullback for the Baltimore Ravens when they won the Super Bowl in 2000, was one of my clients. This year the Ravens' cheerleaders have just committed me for the third year as their nutritionist. And I will tell you there are worse groups to hang out with.

Again, I am very honored and privileged to have worked with these people. I'll have to say that to work with the athletes and to have obtained that reputation is wonderful and I really enjoy it. However, about ninety percent of my time is spent right here in my office working with people just like us who want to look good, feel good, and maybe most importantly, show the results of their exercise program. The real positive here is that I'm capable of taking world class, cutting edge, scientifically proven information and tailor it to the day-to-day life of anyone who needs my assistance. I can make this program fit anyone! I learned a long time ago to build my life and career on an ethical foundation. The stones of that foundation are honesty, character, integrity (which isn't a big word in my business, unfortunately), faith and loyalty. The cover of the nutrition manual I provide to my clients says, "To be honest, caring, and compassionate about what you do, to know that it is right, and that it makes a life-changing difference. There is no greater reward in this life."

Wright

What would you say sets you apart from other nutritionists, dieticians, or the proverbial mass marketed diet gurus?

Swinney

One of the bigger things is that I do not, cannot, and have not ever implemented a one-size-fits-all mass marketed nutrition philosophy. I pride myself in being able to work with each person as an individual with his or her own particular needs, wants, goals, and desires in mind. This is a very common sense program that it is very easy to do.

I have to say I don't even like the word "diet." Mom always said that four-letter words are ugly words, so diet is the D word. If you look at it closely and break it down the first three letters spell "die," and that should bother us just a little bit. A lifestyle change that includes starvation, deprivation, and restriction is not a lifestyle change at all and not something we can live with over the long haul. I like to have my clients eat plenty of good food; we have tons of recipes they can use. My wife, Kristen, and I are currently working on our own cookbook which we are excited about. I give people permission to eat and enjoy food. I don't like to use the word "fail," but the only way anyone can fail on this type nutrition program is to not eat! That makes my program radically and dramatically different from any of the unhealthy, mass-marketed "short-term fixes" we see that are being shoved down our throats on a regular basis.

Wright

That really sounds good! Who would you say your programs are practical for?

Swinney

That is a good question and I can give a brief answer to that—anyone and everyone. This has been a hobby of mine for more than twenty-five years now. It has been my career—for fifteen years, after all this time, I can tell you very emphatically I have never met anyone I could not help. It doesn't matter if he or she is an athlete or not. It doesn't matter if he or she exercises or not, young or old, or fit or fat, and quite frankly I have seen all of the above. I guess the bottom line is everyone can be better and throughout the course of my program we will find the right things for that particular person so this program is in fact suitable for anyone and everyone—the world class athletes, the clinically obese, those with health concerns, and eating disorders. I think I can handle any kind of problem people face, and handle it in a safe, healthy manner that produces their desired result.

Wright

What could one expect by following your guidelines or being under your guidance?

Swinney

There are a variety of things that could happen. Number one, we like to keep steady blood sugar levels throughout the course of the day. As a result of that, energy levels will be more constant, more consistent and all around better! There will be none of the unpleasant, uncomfortable, unproductive "low blood sugar blues," that causes headaches, dizziness, nausea, and blurred vision, among other things, we want to avoid anything unpleasant all cost.

I am probably the most hard-core guy you will ever meet when it comes to losing muscle—we don't like losing muscle, and on my program the individual will gain muscle. Muscle is metabolically active, it is a living breathing tissue and that is why I say there is no coincidence that the first three letters in word diet is "d-i-e." When you diet and your body senses deprivation, famine, and restriction you will burn off your muscle tissue before you tap into stored body fat. When that happens you are literally killing off that living breathing tissue. Parts of you are literally dieing at that point in time. A pound of muscle will burn 18,000 to 20,000 calories a year more than a pound of fat. A five-pound muscle gain will allow you to burn an extra 275 calories per day without even changing your activity level! Conversely, losing muscle brings your metabolism and fat burning mechanisms to a screeching halt!

Eighty-five percent of my time is spent doing body fat reduction programs, and I get very specific about body *fat* not body *weight*. We want to be sure we are losing fat. We can loose weight by cutting out water for a day or two or starving ourselves but we didn't do anything healthy or productive, or anything that will last, so focusing on body fat is of fundamental importance. Most importantly we have to realize that general health is a great concern—we don't do anything unhealthy at all. We always want health to improve and it will, just as a byproduct of everything else we're doing.

Wright

You call your program "Metabolism Building Nutrition." Would you give us an overview of nutrition done that way?

Swinney

I think that is a real interesting and very accurate term. Let's take the word "metabolism" and define it for a moment. To put it in simple terms, your metabolism is that array of chemical processes in your body that dictates how efficiently you process nutrients, build muscle, and burn fat. What we want to focus on is getting the metabolism more active and more efficient in those three areas.

If we were to think back to our days in junior high school, high school, and perhaps our first few years of college, our friends, acquaintances, and classmates at the time who had weight problems on the heavy end of the scale, we would find they were the exception not the rule. This is because we had a high metabolism going for us through puberty, adolescence, and on into our teens and early twenties. We could stand at the refrigerator with both arms going and practically never gain an ounce, regardless of what we were scarfing down!

Well, I am forty-two at this point, not twenty-two, and I can tell you, our metabolism changes as we age—that is the fact of it. We don't have to grow up necessarily and I refuse to; but we do age a little and our metabolism is something that definitely slows down as we age. My focus is to get the metabolism revved up just as much as possible and make anyone more efficient once again at doing the things the body does naturally.

Of fundamental importance in metabolism building nutrition is getting enough complete protein. What most people misunderstand is that protein, second only to water, is the most abundant nutrient in the human body. Protein is not bad or harmful, it is our healing nutrient and it is found in every cell in your body. Most people eat too little quality protein. There are two interesting facts about protein: 1) It is the last thing your body can convert to fat, and 2) Protein is our metabolically active nutrient. When we eat protein our metabolic rate goes up higher—up to seventy percent—and stays up longer than with either fats or carbs. We like to choose good lean, complete protein sources when on a program designed to build your metabolism, build muscles, and burn stored body fat. Lean protein sources would include egg whites because we can significantly reduce the fat by removing some of the yolks. Eggs are a convertible food in that manner; you can use the whites only or whites and a few of the egg yolks or egg substitutes, and there are many good brands. Lean protein sources also include white meat chicken, white meat turkey, tuna, and white meat fish. The darker meat fish are a little higher in fat content and even though that fat has some healthy attributes we would limit it initially. Other lean meats are shellfish such as shrimp, scallops, lobster, crab, mussels, and clams. One of my favorite meals is a huge plate—the biggest plate you have ever seen—full of nice steamed shrimp. I can sit there and peel and eat shrimp until I can't move and know that I didn't do anything wrong—it feels like a treat.

Next would be the starchy carbohydrates. We have been brutally, horribly misled into believing that carbohydrates are awful, evil, horrible, nasty, ugly fat producing foods, and I have to tell you that is just not true. Foods in the carbohydrate class are your fuel source. They are the cleanest burning source of fuel you can put into your body. If you have ever tried a low carb or no carb diet, then you have discovered just how unpleasant that really is. If you have any activity level at all you can't run on empty—you just can't. Carbs are very important. The real misunderstanding is that most people eat the wrong type of carbs at the wrong time of day.

There is a reason we pull into the filling station and fill the tank with gas when the car's gas gauge indicates it's near empty. We know that when the tank is empty that car, truck, or SUV is not going to take us any farther. Your body can't take you any farther either if you are trying to run on empty. There is a great list of good, starchy carbohydrates that we like to utilize on this program. Oatmeal is a great starter in the morning. Other good fuels include things like: Cream of Wheat, cream of rice, grits—all those things are just fine. Other foods in that category are: brown rice, wild rice, corn, beans (all beans), peas, potatoes, sweet potatoes, just any type of an unrefined grain. We have been mislead about these things and it is time we understand foods in the carbohydrate food group are our fuel sources, nutrient dense and doing without them is unpleasant and unproductive at best.

Now, we don't over-shoot the fuel value. When we stop at the filling station and the gas pump clicks off and the tank is full, we don't continue to squeeze the pump handle and let the fuel run out on the ground. That wouldn't be good, especially with the price of gas today. We want to do the same thing with your body. We want to make sure you're fueled for your activity level but we don't want to over-shoot your fuel needs. This is really a very, very easy thing to keep in check and is not confusing or difficult at all.

Next we have another food group that I refer to as fibrous carbohydrates. Fibrous carbohydrates are just as the name applies—they have a higher fiber content and because the weight of fibrous foods are made up of more water and fiber, they don't give us the same energy or fuel value as we get from the starchy carbs.

Remember, protein doesn't give you a fuel yield like starch, also, the fibrous carbs don't give you the same fuel yield. So fibrous carbs and protein are the two food groups that we don't need to worry about over-consuming in regards to body fat. The benefit of the fibrous carbs is, of course, in part the high fiber content, which we know is important for a healthy digestive system. We've heard that for years and years. For our purpose, for metabolism building nutrition however, the fibrous carbs slow down our rate of digestion, which facilitates uptake of the various nutrients, glucose and amino acids from each meal.

Fibrous carbs include: asparagus, broccoli, Brussel sprouts, cabbage, cauliflower, carrots, egg plant, green beans, kale, leeks, mushrooms, okra, onions, spinach, squash, zucchini—just anything you can think of that you would put in a salad. You just can't eat too many lean, cruciferous, fibrous carbs.

Now we want to look at a list of foods we would want to avoid on a program of metabolism building nutrition. We know that there is a long list of dietary fats—saturated fats—that convert to body fat very readily, so we want to avoid them. Included in this are: red meat, butter, margarine, egg yolks, oils and anything else we know is high fat.

Next we really want to watch the simple sugars that also convert to fat very readily. The thing that most people misunderstand is we think a calorie is a calorie, is a calorie. Not true! All calories *are not* created equal! If someone has a whole lot of body fat to lose we very often temporarily limit and sometimes totally eliminate dairy products, fruits, and fruit juices. Now those are not unhealthy things by any stretch of the imagination, but if we eliminate them for a brief period of time we can certainly speed up fat loss by losing the simple sugars that are prominent in these foods.

For example milk—even skim milk that has no fat—has a very high sugar content. That sugar is called lactose. Fruits and fruit juices have been referred to as nature's candy and I think that's an accurate description. The sugar in those foods is called fructose. What most people don't understand about fructose is that it converts to a fat or a triglyceride in your liver before it is ever released into your blood stream. As a result you can't use it as a fuel source, you can't burn it off—it is never going to give you energy—but rather it is always stored as a fat. Again fruit is healthy but we would like to focus more on lower fructose, higher fiber fruits. In this category are: green apples or granny smith apples; any of the berries such as blackberries, raspberries, strawberries, blueberries, boysenberries—the berries are just great.

When you realize this wide variety of foods we can have you see that restriction and deprivation really aren't part of the program; and you can take this as far as you want it to go. I know people are tired of hearing the term "lifestyle change" but this really is that lifestyle change we have been looking for. Balance is a good point of focus. No "fad" diet has ever offered balance.

If we take a step back and just glance over this whole program, the foods that we eat are already naturally fat free, they are already naturally sugar free, they are not processed, they are nutrient dense, and they are metabolically active. Unprocessed and in their natural state is the way they were put on planet earth and intended for human consumption. No smoke, no mirrors, no magic, just eat good lean clean nutrient dense, metabolically active foods and this will in fact change your life.

Wright

How quickly does an individual respond to your nutrition program, and what kind of results could an individual expect?

Swinney

I can tell you I have seen every kind of result in the world. I have seen just about anything you would want to see and I have seen a whole lot of things you might not want to see! With a genetically gifted, world-class athlete or with a bodybuilder before competition, if they are local and they come to my office every week, it is because we want a change in muscle gain and fat loss on a weekly basis, and we get it!

The bodybuilders are the best group in the world when it comes to building muscle and losing fat. Not everyone fits into that category. I can tell you that I have personally witnessed individuals with slow metabolisms and the clinically obese lose 150 pounds of body fat in a year's time. As a conservative guess, I like to see fat loss of somewhere around a half pound to a pound a week per 100 pounds of body weight. I like to see a muscle gain of half to three quarters of a pound per a week and there again I am being conservative. I have seen people loose fifteen to twenty pounds of body fat in a month's time and be able to stay consistent with that over the long haul. Remember too, I chart their progress via regular body composition testing so we're sure to lose fat, not muscle.

People on my program have multiple visits—I see people on a regular basis because, 1) I want to know I am doing the right thing for them, 2) that their body is responding favorably and very positively to what we are doing, and 3) we know there are plateaus—times when you will hit that proverbial wall. When that happens we want to adjust and change things so you can keep responding in a very positive and favorable manner all the way through the program.

Wright

We are bombarded with tons of diet information. Would you dispel for our readers any diet myths?

Swinney

The first thing I have to say is there is no such thing as a short-term quick fix. Secondly I would say diet, which we have already talked about. Look at the first three letters that spell d-i-e. When we think about diet we as average Americans think about depravation, restriction, and starvation. Honestly, diets are something we are not supposed to stick to and most of them don't work anyway. If they did then we probably wouldn't even be having this conversation and I wouldn't be contributing to this book. Many of the diets out there are even unhealthy. We have even resorted to things as severe as gastric bypasses when it comes to body modification. That's too extreme and unhealthy. There is a twenty percent mortality rate with that surgery. Would we take that risk anywhere else in life?

Wright

I had a good friend die as a result of a gastric bypass.

Swinney

That is excess. We just need to change our thinking about food. We need to quit relying on the uneducated, mass marketed diet gurus, reading a book, or implementing those unhealthy programs and think it is going to be the solution for the long term. Again, let's just go back to metabolism building nutrition, and look at these good, lean, clean nutrient dense metabolically active foods. As I said they were put on planet earth in this form already unaltered. Gosh I would just have to sum it up and say once again that diets don't work. The yo-yo diet syndrome in the United States right now is completely out of control and made us more obese as a society than ever before!

In the year 2003 obesity was the second leading cause of death in the United States next to tobacco related illnesses. That should shake us up more than just a little bit. The only positive note is it does let me know that I am going to have a job for a while! I'm joking about that of course, but that really should bother us. The reason is simply because we make the wrong choices. It's not because we are overeating. It is not the quantity of the food but the quality of the food, so don't fall into the diet trap, please stay away from that.

Wright

If you were to summarize and give our readers and listeners some tips for success, what would you say to them?

Swinney

We can make this real simple and actually someone could implement this program from just looking at what I am going to say here. First of all we want to choose nutrient dense metabolically active food, the ones we talked about earlier. With each meal we want to choose something out of the lean protein, the starchy carbohydrate, and the fibrous carbohydrate groups. We want to avoid the fats and the sugars I mentioned. We also need to realize calories aren't bad, calories are good but all calories are not created equal. Protein does one thing, starchy carbohydrates do another, fibrous carbohydrates do yet something else, and fats again are totally different as are the simple sugars and alcohol.

There are only four things in nature that yield a calorie. Protein, carbohydrates, fats, or alcohol and everything is going to fall into those categories, so realize that it is the quality of the calorie not the quantity of the calorie.

I often ask people in my office if they can define a calorie. I get a puzzled look from them and I say, "Let me define it for you. The medical book says it is the amount of heat necessary to raise one gram of water one degree Celsius. Does that mean anything to you?" Well, I can tell you after fifteen years in this career it still doesn't mean anything to me. I have never had anyone set a pot of water on my head and try to raise it a degree, so I don't even know if that is an accurate definition anymore; but that is the way it is defined in the medical books—a meaningless definition to everyone I know.

Most of my clients will eat from four to seven meals per a day, depending on their schedule. Now for the fifth, sixth, and seventh meals we are looking more at the athletes; but four and five meals is very common for the average person. We want to eat regularly and consistently throughout the day so that we keep the blood sugar levels steady and we are constantly giving our bodies a supply of those good, lean, clean, lean, nutritious foods. "Grazing" is a pretty good word here. Eating that way keeps you revved up more than you have ever been revved up before in regards to your metabolism.

Exercise is also a fundamental component in body modification. Get some cardiovascular exercise and progressive resistance training, or weight training and you'll be happy with those results. Don't ever be hungry that is unpleasant and uncomfortable as well as unproductive. It is something we never ever have to do. I would not ever want any of my clients to draw a hungry breath—that just won't work.

I am just like anyone else, when I get hungry I am going to eat the first thing that doesn't eat me first and that is bad. So don't be hungry—eat at regular intervals throughout the course of the day and you'll avoid cravings. Realize too that supervision and guidance are good things. It is okay to seek assistance in certain areas of your life. If you are on your way to see me for an appointment and your car breaks down, please call me. I will come get you and I will bring you here and we will finish the appointment. But when I get there don't pop the hood and say, "Hey Todd what do you think about this noise under here?" You'd better call a mechanic for that. You put me under your hood and you are going to have a worse problem than you did before your car ever broke down to start with. I don't call the plumber when the power goes out and I don't call the electrician for a leaky sink! Too often we are guilty though of taking "diet" advice from anyone and everyone! More so than on any other topic, everyone is a self-proclaimed nutritionist and they know what works! So we all have our specialties.

Seek the supervision and guidance of a qualified professional for whatever it is you are looking for. Lastly, and most importantly, if you want to change, be held accountable to yourself. You shouldn't participate in a program to make *me* happy, you can't participate in my program to make your husband, wife, training partner, brother, sister, aunt, uncle, girlfriend, or boyfriend happy. This is something you will have to want to do for yourself. Another point of being held accountable, and I think this is rather comical—I ask it of people all the time—have you ever eaten anything by accident? I can tell you for a fact that I have never done that (except for that fraternity initiation in college which I did not have anything to do with). Everything that has made its way into our bodies we've made a conscious decision to pick up, put it in our mouth, chew, and swallow. If we've made the wrong decision then it can take us somewhere we don't want to go.

Let me just close by saying if you are unhappy with who you are or where you are don't worry—don't stress over it, don't even fret about it—because you do not have to stay there. If you don't like what you've gotten out of your body, you simply have to change what you put into it! Garbage in; garbage out. That's the simple harsh fact. I think that is a pretty profound statement and summarizes my program very nicely.

Wright

Today we have been talking to Todd Swinney. Since he was a teenager he envisioned establishing a fitness center with a full functioning nutritional center as part of the operation. Today even more than ever, Todd is convinced that nutrition is seventy-five percent of the equation when it comes to changing your body. Listening to him today I think I agree with him; at least he makes sense to me.

Todd, thank you so much for being with us today. I know you have taken time out of your busy schedule and I want you to know how much I appreciate it.

Swinney

Well, it has been a sincere pleasure and a dream come true for me to participate in *The Game Matters*.

Wright

Thank you so much for being with us on T*he Game Matters*.

About The Author

Todd Swinney became involved in the sport of bodybuilding in 1978 and was an active competitor from 1980 until 1990. In 1990, Todd took his hobby of twelve years and formed a career in nutrition counseling and professional fitness training. Todd is considered one of the top authorities in his sport and has, fortunately for all of us, built a business by taking his level of cutting edge, scientifically proven nutrition information and tailoring it to the day-to-day life of any individual who has the desire to lose body fat, gain muscular bodyweight or address health concerns. Todd's clients range from professional athletes to the clinically obese and anything in between. The year 2005 is the third year that Todd is the nutritionist for the Baltimore Ravens Cheerleaders. There are too many other celebrity athletes to even mention here. Todd is the Chairman of the Maryland District of the National Physique Committee of the USA and has been a judge with that organization since 1988. Currently Todd works his nutrition magic from his office, "ELITE IMAGE NUTRITION" in Millersville, Maryland.

Todd Swinney

Phone: 410.729.0005

Fax 410.729.0546

Email: Todd@ToddSwinney.com

www.toddswinney.com

www.beverlyintl.com